Getting More
from
Your Bible Reading

John Alan Carlson

BETHANY HOUSE PUBLISHERS
MINNEAPOLIS, MINNESOTA 55438
A Division of Bethany Fellowship, Inc.

Published by Bethany House Publishers
A Division of Bethany Fellowship, Inc.
6820 Auto Club Road, Minneapolis, Minnesota 55438

Printed in the United States of America

Library of Congress Cataloging in Publication Data

Carlson, John Alan, 1951-
   Getting more from your Bible reading.

   Includes bibliographical references.
    1. Bible—Criticism, interpretation, etc.
2. Bible—Study. I. Title
BS511.2.C37 1982   220.6'01   82-14563
ISBN O-87123-256-1 (pbk.)

DEDICATION

To the Church, passionately loved by Christ;
And to my own bride, a sterling example
of Christian womanhood.

THE AUTHOR

John Alan Carlson came to Christ as a collegian during the "Jesus Movement." He received the B.A. degree summa cum laude and is an accomplished violinist. A piano tuner and rebuilder, he soon acquired a piano store. He was eventually appointed a Bible teacher and then an elder in his church. Carlson, his wife and two children now live near Boston, MA. He is enrolled in the M.Div. program at Gordon-Conwell Theological Seminary.

ACKNOWLEDGMENTS

I imagine that one's first book is always the hardest. Looking back on the course of writing this one, I can see that it never could have arrived at its present form apart from the help, the sacrifice, the guidance and the prayers of many people. It's only right to give credit to those most directly involved. Many thanks to *Decision* magazine's School of Christian Writing for the invaluable shove in the right direction; to our critique group for the prize-winning insights which gave the book its character (my wife, Barb, Steve Snyder, Mark and Mona Nelson); to Jim and Mary Amundson for their generous help and encouragement; to Sue Peterson for her typing; and to the many others who encouraged and prayed—and waited. The Lord who ordained the book gave grace to all!

FOREWORD

Hermeneutics involves interpreting or explaining a written document—ancient or contemporary. When interpreting the Bible, we can make this process too easy or we can make it too difficult. There are many factors involved in interpreting the Bible. We need to know what any passage meant to the first hearers or reader, and we need to know if and how we should use or apply the passage today. If we should *not* apply the passage, we need to know why we should not. And if we *should* apply it, we want to make the right application.

The author of this book gets to the heart of the problem for many Bible students. He points out that some students of the Bible have no confidence in their own ability to interpret correctly and are therefore fearful. This is often true of young, new Christians. Others—often older Christians and lay leaders or pastors—simply depend on their well-known trusty commentaries and other sources and rarely make any fresh discoveries of truth.

John Alan Carlson here points the way for all Bible students to have a growing, fresh experience in their Bible study. His procedures are easy to follow. He recognizes both the human side of the Bible and its divine side. He wants Bible study to transform our lives, not simply to inform our minds.

This is a good book for all students who want to be "doers of the message and not hearers only." Those who are only hearers "deceive themselves [by merely hearing]" (James 1:22; cf. Matt. 7:26). If we are to be doers of the message of God, we need to understand the message, make the message a part of ourselves, and live it out day by day.

—A. Berkeley Mickelson
Professor of New Testament Interpretation,
Bethel Theological Seminary

TABLE OF CONTENTS

Chapter 1

Music of the Master

Perhaps you have also marveled, as I often have, at how easy it is to tell a student violinist from a master. They may both be able to play all the notes in time and in tune, and yet the master possesses the peculiar ability to make the music come alive. His sensitivity to each note gives the music a magical quality all its own that seemingly comes out of nowhere. You wonder how he does it; and yet it appears as effortless as breathing for him, as if he would say that the music came alive all by itself. And you can only imagine that, somehow, he knew the heart of the composer intimately, and understood firsthand just how every phrase and innuendo was intended to contribute to the whole.

A student, on the other hand, may succeed *technically* in everything—playing in tune, making diminuendos where he should, and so on. And yet, the music gives no illusion of "coming alive" the way it does when played by a master. At best, it seems a little dry, and at worst, laborious and tiring—for both performer and listener. You are very conscious of the student's great effort to do everything he has been taught to do. But the music itself, as the composer conceived it, never seems to find its way to the surface.

11

Though he may have played perfectly, you sense that something is missing. Somehow, an intuitive grasp of the music itself still eludes him.

There is a striking difference between the student and the master—a distance that the student has yet to go, or a hurdle that he has yet to leap. He may be preoccupied with the technical challenge of the violin; he may need to learn more or perhaps just mature as a musician. But for some reason, he has not yet reached beyond the jungle of printed musical notations to the tenderness of Grieg's heart, or to the fire in Liszt's heart, or the grandeur in Brahms'. Many students, to be sure, never reach that far beyond the printed page. But by the same token, every master was first a student who had to wrestle with the basics of technique and theory. No one, contrary to popular myth, has ever been born with mastery of the violin.

If I were writing to violin students, it would be to help them over their "hurdle" and send them on their way to true master-level playing. But I write instead to fellow Christians who are experiencing a similar frustration—*their Bible reading.* They are wondering: *Why doesn't it come alive?*

By comparing the Bible with music, I believe we can better understand the nature of the "hurdle" that we as Christians face, and also how to overcome it. How do we study the scriptures to discover what a passage means? How do we find the "flow"? And even more important, how can we reach beyond the printed page of scripture to the heart of God?

We just considered a student violinist. Now let's consider two Christians with similar difficulties. Lynn began studying the Bible as a new believer and was soon overwhelmed by the magnitude of the task before her. She was temporarily rescued by some study guides her pastor recommended which gave her a good start in understanding basic doctrines. But she is no longer a novice and still finds herself dependent upon prepared Bible studies. And they no longer satisfy her growing hunger for God's deeper message that she senses is contained in Scripture. But she gets little out of her independent reading and study because she doesn't trust her own ideas and insights. She reasons to herself that since great theologians and experienced ministers have disagreed on interpretations, who am I that I should understand the Bible correctly? Her real problem is that she never learned how to test her own ideas and insights. She doesn't know how to form reliable conclusions or find the answers to questions herself.

Richard, an experienced pastor, has a different problem. He is quite skilled at church administration, counseling and sermon preparation. And he seems to know his Bible so well that he never finds anything new in it. He has to pour such immense energy to extract one new particle of inspiring insight that it hardly seems worth the effort. His library already contains a complete outline and explanation of his church's doctrine in addition to all the sermon ideas he could ever use. "Besides," he reasons, "pastors have a lot of responsibilities other than Bible study. It's just not worth all that effort. My library will have to do." His real problem is that he does not perceive the inexhaustible depth and riches of the scriptures. He got stuck somewhere between the history and the dogmatics and never learned how to dig deeper to discover the heart of God in it all.

But many people have discovered the heart of God in seemingly exhausted portions of their Bibles, and those passages have suddenly become the most exciting. For there's nothing more desirable to man than the heart of God, when you perceive it with *your* heart.

It's the same as how a master violinist makes music exciting by reaching beyond the printed music to the heart of the composer. And here is where the student violinist still falls short. His playing is essentially secondhand. He diligently does what he has been taught, exactly as the music notation directs, while lacking that firsthand understanding of the music itself that translates so readily into the feelings of the composer.

Our two Bible students have the same secondhand syndrome. Lynn doesn't trust her own insights, while Richard never seems to *have* any of his own. They both fall short of a firsthand understanding of the Bible because they haven't discovered for themselves the heart of God permeating each passage. And as a result, their personal Bible reading remains stifled.

Why is a firsthand grasp of the Bible's message so vital? To begin with, the Bible is a meeting place in our relationship with God. In a time of devotional reading, God desires both to speak to us and to reveal himself to us. I could tell you that God comforts the sorrowing. But it would be so much better if in a time of loneliness, you lifted your own eyes to God for comfort and then read, " 'Lo, I am with you always, even to the end of the age,' "[1] and then found your heart flooded with assurance from God that He was present and was concerned for you.

Likewise, I could tell you that God provides for His children. But how much better that in a time of need you confess your worries to God and read in Hebrews 13:5, " 'I will never desert you, nor will I ever forsake you.' " And then as the needs are met, you find in your heart a humble gratitude reflecting the knowledge that this was no accident; your heavenly Father really was caring for you. A relationship is growing! And this could never happen secondhand.

Also, firsthand discovery is the best way to learn. For when we discover something ourselves, we gain knowledge with understanding and with personal depth—and therefore, permanence! Reference books are useful, but they can't possibly answer all our questions, and *every* human teacher is fallible. Infallibility is not our goal either, of course; the heart of God is our goal. And that simply *cannot be perceived secondhand!*

Also very basic is the fact that the Church, Christ's body, will be greatly strengthened as many Christians become truly competent to handle the scriptures. In fact, this is essential for the Church to fulfill her mission here on earth. It is a primary weapon of our warfare.[2] So let us become equipped![3]

As mentioned earlier, the secret of personal Bible study lies in searching out the heart of God in what we read. It is there, underlying every passage, energizing every verse, carrying each book. It is the lifeblood of Scripture!

Here is where the Bible and music are most wonderfully alike. In great music, there is a mysterious flowing quality that seems almost to have a soul of its own. Somehow, the composer put something of his own heart into the music that revives every time it is played. Each note contributes to it, and a fine performing musician intuitively understands just how *each note* can best enhance the whole.

And so it is with the Bible. Underneath all the history, admonitions and teaching of the Bible, there pulsates the lifegiving Spirit of God with a particular flow of revelation and purpose for each book. This "lifeblood" is the burden of God's heart that caused that book to be born! And discovering it is like discovering the treasure hid in a field! The book becomes yours forever, because you have found its very cornerstone deep in God's heart. Every detail and every aspect of that book work together to express that burden, just like the many notes in a symphony. And once you discern this "lifeblood" of a book of scripture, you can weigh all questions or possible interpretations of that book against its proper foundation—the heart of God.

But most important, you will have become better acquainted with God for your discovery, and your deepened understanding of His heart will enhance your spiritual life and your understanding of all scripture.

Now, how do we overcome this "hurdle"? How do we become mature in our handling of scripture and sensitive to God's heart throughout? Assuming someone is willing to do the necessary work, is there a method or procedure that is guaranteed to help him become intimate with scripture?

There is most definitely a guarantee of success, but not lying in any particular method. It lies only in the diligent application of the basic *principles of Bible study*. Methods are normally designed to meet a specific goal or overcome a particular problem, but *principles are universal*. And although all good methods are built on the same inviolable principles, it is possible to use a good method and fall short due to unconscious neglect of one of those principles.

To illustrate, let's consider again the study of the violin. There are many good and successful methods; some are exercise books, others consist of more comprehensive disciplines of practice and attitude. And each is designed with particular problems and goals in mind. But behind every method are the same working principles such as the dynamics of tone production and proper hand and wrist positions. If a student learns and applies them, he will make rapid progress toward his goal. Guaranteed. But if, for example, he neglects proper left-hand position while practicing, he will make little if any progress. But the exercise book is not at fault here. An underlying principle has been neglected.

Likewise in the study of the Bible, there are many different methods, such as character study, book study, through the Bible in one year, and so on (see Supplement A). But there are principles which underlie every sound method. If you learn and apply them, you are likewise guaranteed to become mature in your handling of scripture; if you neglect any one of them, no method will work for you.

For example, if you undertake a word study and neglect the "translational barrier," you could work hard and make little progress, not to mention the possible mistakes. Suppose for a moment that you wanted to trace the word "deliver" through a portion of the Bible with only a translation. Your results would depend entirely upon which translation you used. And if, for example, you used the King James Version, how could you know that twenty-five different Hebrew and Greek words are represented by the same English word "deliver"? You wouldn't know which particular word was being used in each case, or what its shades of meaning might be. And how many times might you overlook *the same words* only because they were translated "help" or "save" or "rescue"? It's possible to make gross errors using this careless type of study, but the fault does not lie with "word study" itself. A principle has been neglected.

If, on the other hand, you understand the "translational barrier," these dangers would be obvious to you, and you wouldn't think of undertaking a word study without a good concordance which identifies the words of the original language and a dictionary or lexicon which defines them. Not only do these tools contain the information you need for accuracy, but knowing how to use them properly makes such a study quite easy!

And since the same principles undergird all methods, a good understanding of the principles will enable you to derive maximum benefit from any method you may use. Even methods that failed you in the past may work well for you when you see beyond their mechanics to their operating principles.

The versatility of a principle is amazing. It not only applies equally to every method, but also to every level of study, to every person and to every portion of scripture. But the greatest single reason for learning principles is that they will guide you as securely as possible—and as quickly as possible—to the "lifeblood" of every passage in the Bible: *the heart of God.* Guaranteed.

Chapter 2

To the Composer's Heart in Three Easy Principles

How do we study the Bible to discover what a passage means? And how do we reach beyond the printed page of scripture to the heart of God? *We ask the right questions!*

For a scientist, a detective, or a tax auditor, the success of his investigation depends entirely upon his ability to ask the right questions, and of course to answer those questions by careful observation. An investigation may spring out of only one question, like "Whodunit?" or "How old is this rock?" But since the answer is impossible to determine directly, what follows is a series of preliminary questions. Observations then give rise to more questions until finally the answer sought becomes apparent. Failing to ask the right questions may result in missing a critical piece of information. And this could cause an entire investigation to fail, while asking key questions right away brings about success as quickly as possible. Good questions are therefore the most basic investigative tool. And to be prepared for Bible study, we must be equipped with some good preliminary questions for whatever we read.

Although it may take a lifetime to develop the art of

asking questions, the technique can be applied to Bible study directly by means of three principles. In fact, the principles are most useful when expressed as questions themselves.

The first principle then is, *"What does it say?"*

Now, that may seem like an embarrassingly simple question, but unfortunately it is often stumbled over. And its most common neglect lies simply in careless reading.

A fifth-grade Sunday school class I once taught memorized Matthew 1:21:"'. . . you shall call His name Jesus, for it is He who will save His people from their sins.' " And after they successfully recited it in unison, I asked them, "What does Jesus save us from?" Nobody knew.

I'm sure every Sunday school teacher has at least one such story to tell. Few people are able to fully grasp the flow of thought in a complex paragraph with just a single reading. And yet, how often do we read a section of scripture without going back to check the logical progression of what we just read? Obvious violators are readers who stop one day at the end of a chapter and resume at a later date without even checking back to refresh their memories. An analytical reader quickly discovers that most chapter divisions in the Bible do not reflect units of thought so much as length. And in most books he finds an unbroken progression of thought from beginning to end. This should tell us how much we are missing when we try to "speed read" the Bible. We need to read carefully, constantly asking ourselves questions to make sure we understand what we are reading. This discipline is called inductive study,[1] and its purpose is to help us thoroughly answer the question, "What does it say?"

But there are several other matters that complicate the question somewhat. We always face the "translational barrier," and occasionally some confusion over the cultural implications of biblical times. We must deal with concepts of prophetic vision, symbolism and parables, and learn to distinguish spiritual reality from physical reality. In short, this first question encompasses all aspects of what we frighteningly call *hermeneutics* (the science of interpretation—it seeks to identify and overcome all interpretive barriers so that we may understand what a writer was actually saying). However, we can stay calmly on the track if we do not lose sight of the essential question, "What does it say?" That is the only question we need to answer at this point. And if various issues of culture or symbolism do not affect that answer, then they can safely be ignored for the present, and possibly forever. But no matter how simple or complex it may be, this question must always be answered first: "What does it say?"

The question effectively guides our study; it challenges us to do the necessary work while at the same time saving us from pointless detours. But besides being an effective tool, it is also very powerful, for it answers the question, "What does it *mean*?" If we are sure that we know exactly what the Bible really does say, then we also know what it means, for God, the Author, is strongly disposed toward saying what He means. Why, after all, should He have any reason to say otherwise? Consider it seriously. "Our God is in the heavens; He does whatever He pleases" (Ps. 115:3). If He already does whatever He pleases, could He ever possibly have any *reason* to lie to man? No. " 'God is not a man, that He should lie' " (Num. 23:19). And so interpretation of the Bible essentially begins and ends with the question, "What does it say?" The second and third questions are therefore designed to deepen and to confirm (or correct) our answers to the first.

The second principle is, *"Does it harmonize and flow?"*
Music harmonizes and flows. At least it used to. Today some music screams and convulses. But the Bible is like good music. It has harmony and flow, and you can expect to find it as you study. It *harmonizes* by presenting many

different perspectives on the same truth with no contradiction, and it *flows* by developing themes logically and revealing truth progressively. The Holy Spirit who inspired all scripture never rambled. Although the various writers of scripture could not have grasped all that God was saying, they were obedient and wrote their burden from God. And through them the Holy Spirit spoke His burden profoundly and perfectly. So, besides the perfect harmony, there is always a clear direction, a definite underlying flow to every passage of scripture. The Bible is such beautiful music! As you read the Bible, ask "Does it harmonize and flow?"

If we are diligent to ask this question constantly as we study, it will work for us in two important ways. First, it will help confirm, or disprove, our answers to the first question. And learning to test our own understanding by watching for harmony and flow is one of the most valuable skills we can develop as students of the Bible. But the second thing this question does is alert us to the flow of revelation below the surface of what we read and at the same time act as our guide as we explore this realm.

For example, Matthew 12 may appear on the surface to be disjointed and have no flow. What do the various confrontations with Pharisees and family have to do with each other and with Matthew as a whole? That question, based upon principle number two, compels us to study until we recognize this as a phase in the disciples' training where they are being fully reoriented toward their closest personal and social ties. This, of course, is one stage of several that Jesus is guiding them through, and when we recognize this, the logical progression of these events becomes apparent.

In this case, other themes are being simultaneously developed in a progressive manner, and it would be a mistake to assume that this one observation exhausted the passage. For instance, the Pharisees' attacks, the motives behind them, and the methods employed are all working together to develop themes such as the mystery of iniquity, the deadness of the Law without the Spirit, and light's inability to fellowship with darkness. But all of these themes are unfolding together in Matthew, where everything revolves around the establishment of the Kingdom of Heaven on the earth.

If we will diligently ask the question, "Does it harmonize and flow?", then our studying will uncover truths close to God's heart and vital to Christian living. The conflicts recorded in Matthew 12 are identical to the conflicts faced today within the church as the Holy Spirit trains disciples. Only the names have been changed to confuse the unwary. Insights gained from a study of this chapter alone are invaluable to a Christian who is struggling to walk in a full commitment to the lordship of Christ.

The third principle is, *"Do I harmonize and flow?"*

As we read scripture, we should find it flowing and in harmony with itself, but like Matthew 12, it should also harmonize with real day-to-day Christian living. And it should harmonize with the character of God and His revelation of himself in nature. If we perceive this harmony and flow, then we may be encouraged that our understanding of scripture is essentially correct. If, on the other hand, there seems to be no flow and many contradictions, that is a strong indication that our understanding of the Bible is incorrect. Perhaps we have not thoroughly and carefully answered question number one. But it is also possible that the problem lies somewhere else entirely. And since the problem is neither with God nor the Bible, we must look for it by asking the third basic question of Bible interpretation, "Do I harmonize and flow?" Am I in harmony with God and His will, and am I flowing by grace with His Spirit and with His people?

Now, it may appear that we have gotten off the track and are no longer talking about Bible interpretation. But quite the opposite is true. We are just getting to the heart of the matter. No in-depth understanding of the Bible is possible without personally "harmonizing and flowing" with God. In fact, all serious doctrinal error can be traced to neglect of this critical third question. All heresies, pseudo-Christian cults, and other biblical distortions result from approaching scripture with a heart that will not harmonize and flow with what it reads. The scriptures can convert a heart,[2] but a heart can also pervert scripture.[3] It depends upon a person's will.

God's purpose in giving the Bible to man was never to impart all understanding to whomever was curious. His purpose was to call men to himself, and then guide and assist those whose hearts desired to live by His laws and to please Him. And for them, God has reserved eternal rewards.

> "The secret things belong to the Lord our God, but the things revealed belong to us and to our children forever, that we may follow all the words of this law." (Deut. 29:29, NIV)

It stands, therefore, that the Bible ("the things revealed") has accomplished its purpose if it has fed and guided the heart that is hungry for God and for righteousness. And if it completely befuddles those who have no desire to "follow all the words of this law," that bears no ill reflection on the scriptures whatsoever. Rather, it pointedly fulfills them.[4]

We also know that a desire to do God's will gives insight into the scriptures.

> "If any man is willing to do His will, he shall know of the teaching, whether it is of God, or whether I speak from Myself." (John 7:17)

And on the other hand, we know that those who disregard God's Word are heading for deception.

> "But prove yourselves doers of the word, and not merely hearers who delude themselves." (James 1:22)

God even *sends* delusion on those who love wickedness.[5] But He personally explains scripture to those who walk close to Him.[6]

In short, we can expect to understand the Bible properly only to the extent that we flow and desire to flow with God, His will, and His people. Therefore this question becomes paramount: "Do I harmonize and flow?" Neglect of this principle has always been disastrous.

We now see a systematic approach to Bible study beginning to take shape around three basic principles: (1) What does it say?, (2) Does it harmonize and flow?, (3) Do I harmonize and flow? As we proceed to analyze and apply these three principles, it is my prayer that you will grow in your understanding of the Bible, and through that growth be strengthened in your spiritual life.

Principle 1

WHAT DOES IT SAY?

Chapter 3

It's All There in Front of You:
The Discipline of Perception

The treasure hid in scripture, its water of life, is the heart of God. Yet to taste that water, we need to overcome a natural barrier, the barrier of communication. For behind scripture there is a person, God, endeavoring to communicate with another person, you—from His heart to yours, by the written word. Because words alone are limited, God has sent prophets to live His message in the flesh before our eyes. He has also commissioned His Spirit to enlighten our minds and hearts as we read the Bible. But since scripture is basically a Person speaking to another person, its treasure lies immediately beyond the natural barrier of communication.

Communication is both an art and a discipline; and though it is simple, it takes some work. It consists essentially of carefully answering the three questions we developed in chapter two. What does it say? Does it harmonize and flow? And do I harmonize and flow?

But like any true art, it is first a *discipline*. And as we pursue the answer to the first question, we must begin by disciplining ourselves to perceive what is before our eyes.

There is a natural tendency to perceive what we *want* to perceive, and it is astonishing how much that tendency affects our Bible interpretation. We must therefore overcome this and learn to perceive *everything* that is before us and not infer more. This does not hinder imagination or creativity, but it does allow us to *clearly* distinguish between explicit content and inferred meaning. And we must begin with this.

The first major step in understanding the Bible, therefore, is to know that you know what it actually does say! We might simply call that careful reading, but the formal discipline, which is designed to help us determine the exact literal meaning of a passage, is *inductive study*.

Inductive study involves reading on three different levels. The first level is the *casual reading* where we notice primarily those things which we are personally inclined to notice. And at this level, a dozen people might read the same thing and have a dozen different opinions about what the author said.

The next level is *investigation*, where we work to notice every *significant* thing that can be noticed, and to analyze the logical relationship between the things observed. A key to this level of study is our ability to recognize which of our observations are truly significant. This is the bread and butter of inductive study. If the same dozen people followed through to this level of reading, their opinions would level out remarkably.

The third level is *identifying with the writer*, as if we were endeavoring to communicate the same things. Would I have chosen the same illustrations? Would I have structured my logical argument in the same way? And ultimately, if I had written what he wrote, would I be satisfied that I had successfully communicated my burden to my intended audience? Your answers to these questions will indicate how thoroughly you understand what the author was really trying to express.

This third level of reading is effective because the most thorough way to learn something is to have to teach it. Ask any teacher! It can be a humiliating time when a person who feels that he understands something teaches it for the first time. If preparing to teach the material does not expose his flaws in understanding, the students' questions will! And although we do not often have the opportunity to teach something that we read, identifying with the writer provides a similar analytical challenge which can be enormously fruitful.

And this is the endpoint of inductive study. Once we clearly understand what the writer was trying to express, we have attained its goal. But to the Bible student, there remains a further goal. He must recognize that behind each human author, there was a Supreme Author, the Holy Spirit, who gave His burden to the writers to express. And the true Bible student must then obey the Bible until the Holy Spirit's burden becomes his own, and his heart is transformed into God's image. We will discuss this further in chapters seven, eight and nine. But let us proceed to outline the system of inductive study.

After the casual reading is over and initial observations are made, we are faced with the challenge of making every significant observation that we possibly can from what we are studying. Without a doubt, the most effective way to do this is to ask good questions about the passage. Our basic question of course is, "What does it say?" And all other questions which we fashion for the study must help us to answer that basic one.

There are several which are helpful to ask for every passage of scripture.

1) Who is writing to whom?

2) Does he plainly state his purpose for writing that book or passage?

3) What is the emotional tenor of the passage? Does it change anywhere?

4) Is there an obvious structure (not based on chapter divisions)?

5) What is the main point?

6) What is the conclusion?

7) What is the logical progression toward the conclusion?

8) What is the logical structure of the book?

9) Does there seem to be a single climax or turning point in the book?

10) Is there repetition of a particular idea, phrase or word? When does it first occur, and when does it last occur? (This may give clue to structure.)

11) What is the theme of the book? Does every sentence contribute to that theme, or are there portions which do not seem to fit? (Portions which do not seem to fit merit *special* study!)

These questions will help us make many useful observations, but then we must begin asking more specific questions based upon those observations. We shall apply this procedure of questions, observations and new questions to a portion of scripture in the "Questions for Group Discussion" (see Supplement C). If after working through that exercise, the reader desires a more in-depth analysis of inductive study, I highly recommend a book on the subject by William C. Lincoln, *Personal Bible Study*.[1]

The disparity between what is written and what we perceive as we read is certainly the greatest obstacle to our knowledge of scripture. And inductive study is the direct solution to this mountainous problem.

But there is one more disparity which we must overcome, a mole hill by comparison. And that is the difference between what we read in English and what was written in the original languages of scripture—the translational barrier. The reason that the barrier exists at all is that the nature of language makes it impossible for any single translation to be perfect. Fortunately, the excellent translations available today keep that barrier to a minimum. Nevertheless, we must consider the nature of this disparity and how to overcome it.

If we had no translations, the barrier would be enormous. For the Bible was not only written in different languages, but also to different cultures in different historical settings. And in order to read the Bible accurately without the aid of translations, we would not only have to be fluent in those languages, but well informed in the history and culture of biblical times as well. There is far more to translating than taking a Greek-English dictionary and finding out what ἀπόλλυμι means! Unless we choose to become experts, we are wise to leave the work of translating to those who are. But it is still helpful for us to understand the task of translating, for it is a cornerstone in the science of hermeneutics.

Translators have the task of coping with changing language and changing culture. But excellent translations are possible because one thing has not changed at all—human nature! Flesh-and-blood men and women with all their human foibles were speaking from their hearts to other flesh-and-blood men and women—*just like us*. And that's what hermeneutics is all about, person-to-person communication. God's nature has not changed at all either. And that's what Bible study is all about, God speaking to us—today, and until the end of the age.

Having the benefit of excellent translations, we should use them. Several of them! Reading several translations gives us exposure to the various shades of meaning that a passage truly carries, while at the same time protecting us from the possible limitations of a single translation. I have often cringed when hearing otherwise responsible Bible expositors build significant doctrinal statements on prepositions in the Authorized Version, prepositions which do not even appear in the excellent modern translations. This carelessness only indicates that they are relying too much on one translation.

There is also a delightful fringe benefit. The variations in word choice and expression provided by a different translation lend a very welcome freshness to our reading. And the content, rather than the wording, once again becomes prominent. This is especially true when we are studying a passage for the tenth time, and that is a boon to inductive study!

We must choose our translations carefully. Supplement B provides a list of recommended versions. It is helpful to use paraphrases as well as translations, but we should be familiar with the strengths and weaknesses of whatever versions we use.

Where questions of meaning are not adequately answered by comparing versions, Bible dictionaries are quite helpful. They provide information of a cultural and historical nature which helps to clarify the meaning of words as the author intended them. Bible commentaries can also be helpful, especially with the background information they provide.

Another very useful tool is the "exhaustive concordance" such as *Strong's* or the *New American Standard Exhaustive Concordance* (Holman) which enable one to identify the exact word in the original text that corresponds to any word of the King James Version or the New American Standard Bible, respectively. These concordances also include cross-referenced Greek and Hebrew dictionaries which define those words for us. Their only drawback is that the information they so easily provide is purely etymological—that is, it pertains only to the meaning of the word itself and does not offer the broader perspectives provided by a Bible dictionary. Nevertheless, they are very helpful for doing word studies, and are widely used by Bible students at every level.

The translational barrier can be assailed as thoroughly as one may choose. But it never needs to be an obstacle to our understanding of scripture, for the most difficult work has been done for us by experts. And if we will use the simple tools which we have abundantly available, we are well equipped to become intimate with the Bible, and with the God of the Bible—the God of Abraham, the God of David, Elijah, you and me.

Chapter 4

Finding What Is Significant:
The Discipline of Perspective

As we continue to pursue the question, "What does it say?", we find that inductive study, together with the necessary translational tools, enables us to *determine* the exact literal meaning of what the Bible says. But hand in hand with the discipline of perception is the discipline of perspective. This discipline helps us to best *understand* the literal meaning of what the Bible says.

The discipline of perspective begins with *taking the Bible at face value*. Usually this is easy enough, but there are times when our natural minds rebel at the idea. Jesus exposes this difficulty in John 3:12 where He asks Nicodemus, " 'If I told you earthly things and you do not believe, how shall you believe if I tell you heavenly things?' " Our minds always seem to balk at heavenly things.

The psychological difficulty we must overcome is basically a "finite rut." It is often difficult for us to fathom a reality which is beyond the natural world. But there is a spiritual reality, the kingdom of heaven, which Jesus said "is near you."[1] And that makes it doubly difficult to accept. It is hard enough to imagine that " 'you shall see the heav-

34

ens opened, and the angels of God ascending and descending upon the Son of Man.' "[2] But when the sick are healed before our eyes, or the blind regain their sight, our natural mind shouts, "This cannot be!" Concepts of eternity and holiness also defy our finite minds. But we must never let this natural resistance cause us to deny the truth of scripture.

On the other hand, we must be careful never to reject our minds either. They are a vital faculty for discerning truth, and must be used together with our spirits. It is only the "finite rut" which must be broken. To do this, our minds need a whole new set of premises on which to base a logical understanding of the spiritual realm. God gives us those premises in scripture, and we must accept them as fact if we are ever to understand spiritual reality.

For example, we have among the foundational premises of scripture that God's throne is established in righteousness and justice.[3] And yet while contemplating a tragedy, a person may conclude that God isn't fair! In such a case, the person has allowed his finite mind to make a judgment which totally rejects the eternal premises of scripture. Of course he will experience confusion. In the face of traumatic circumstances, it would be far better to affirm the fact of God's righteousness and allow that truth to put the circumstances into a proper perspective.

A second cardinal discipline of perspective is to *focus our attention in scripture on the activity of the heart*. The internal struggles of a man are far more significant than the circumstances which served to generate his crisis. It does not matter so much that David was in a cave hiding from Saul and that Daniel was in a lions' den. What matters is that they were both utterly helpless and cried out only to God for their deliverance. Conversely, it may appear to be a trivial detail that God shut the door to the ark after Noah and his family had entered; but as we contemplate Noah's trauma of heart in gazing for the last time upon the condemned world, it becomes for him a milestone of support.

As we discipline ourselves to read in this way, we often find a much greater flow in scripture. For example, in chapter two we cited the many conflicts of Matthew 12. The circumstances themselves may seem unrelated, but as we focus our attention on the disciples' crisis of heart, we see that Jesus was carefully guiding them through a series of shakings to fulfill the promise He made to them at the end of the previous chapter, " 'You shall find rest for your souls.' " He was delivering them from an enormous amount of oppression and giving them rest. And He was accomplishing that by retraining their hearts and by revealing to them the desires of God's heart.

Through the many conflicts within the bosom of man, the scripture reveals deep secrets of God's purposes and even God's own heart. Though society is complex, and nature is intricate beyond discovery, yet there is nothing in the realm of God's creation as unsearchable as the human heart. And that is where God has staged the true drama of the Bible. We can therefore follow the unfolding of God's revelation in scripture most closely by concentrating our attention on the heart of man, and as it is revealed, the heart of God.

A third discipline of perspective is our *recognition of the writers' familiar surroundings*. When the biblical writers wrote to their immediate audience, they could safely assume a certain mimimum knowledge of local geography, politics, and customs. So we often find references to such things where additional detail would enhance our understanding of the passage, yet no detail is given. Bible atlases are designed to overcome this problem. They range from the dozen or so maps found at the end of many Bibles to excellent books which provide exciting reading in themselves. At times, specific information provided in an atlas may be necessary for a study; at other times, the background information may serve primarily to give us a feel for the setting and perhaps help us to identify more closely with the characters as real people.

A fourth element is our *treatment of symbolic writing*. Three types of biblical writing are highly symbolic: parables, living allegory, and prophetic vision. What characterizes these types of symbolic writing is that the most significant level of truth lies beyond the natural terms in which the message is actually expressed. This in no way means that the passages are untrue, however. Symbolism is simply the written means by which the Holy Spirit has chosen to communicate certain heavenly truths, truths of the spiritual realm which are not readily expressed in natural terms. At times, it is also a means of "sealing" revelation.[4] In other words, He may withhold the interpretation of the symbols until He chooses to reveal the details of the prophetic secret to His servants. In such cases, it is impossible to determine the exact interpretation of a passage before the appointed time when God makes it known.

In the case of *parables*, only the interpretation is really significant. The story itself might well be invented. Consider the parable of the tares.

> He presented another parable to them, saying, "The kingdom of heaven may be compared to a man who sowed good seed in his field. But while men were sleeping, his enemy came and sowed tares also among the wheat, and went away. But when the wheat sprang up and bore grain, then the tares became evident also. And the slaves of the landowner came and said to him, 'Sir, did you not sow good seed in your field? How then does it have tares?' And he said to them, 'An enemy has done this!' And the slaves said to him, 'Do you want us, then, to go and gather them up?' But he said, 'No; lest while you are gathering up the tares, you may root up the wheat with them. Allow both to grow together until the harvest; and in the time of the harvest I will say to the reapers, "First gather up the tares and

bind them in bundles to burn them up; but gather the wheat into my barn."'" (Matt. 13:24-30)

For this parable, Jesus also interprets the symbols.

Then He left the multitudes, and went into the house. And His disciples came to Him, saying, "Explain to us the parable of the tares of the field." And He answered and said, "The one who sows the good seed is the Son of Man, and the field is the world; and as for the good seed, these are the sons of the kingdom; and the tares are the sons of the evil one; and the enemy who sowed them is the devil, and the harvest is the end of the age; and the reapers are angels. Therefore just as the tares are gathered up and burned with fire, so shall it be at the end of the age. The son of Man will send forth his angels, and they will gather out of His kingdom all stumbling blocks, and those who commit lawlessness, and will cast them into the furnace of fire; in that place there shall be weeping and gnashing of teeth. Then the righteous will shine forth as the sun in the kingdom of their Father. He who has ears, let him hear." (Matt. 13:36-43)

Notice that the story is declared at the beginning to be a parable, and notice also the cue, "The kingdom of heaven is like . . . " It doesn't matter much whether or not an actual farmer had an enemy who sowed bad seed among his crops. Jesus is not teaching about farming, He is teaching about the kingdom of heaven. The parable accurately depicts the end of the age; the story of the farmer may be altogether fictional.

For this reason, we must take careful note that the story is declared to be a parable. For we cannot dismiss as fiction whatever *historical* passages may also have symbolic significance! Many stories of scripture have symbolic meaning though they are factual in themselves. These are the *living allegories*.

Consider the story of Hagar and Sarah. They were certainly people, and yet they were also a living allegory. The apostle Paul explains this to us in the book of Galatians.

> For it is written that Abraham had two sons, one by the bondwoman and one by the free woman. But the son by the bondwoman was born according to the flesh, and the son by the freewoman through the promise. This contains an allegory: for these women are two covenants, one proceeding from Mount Sinai bearing children who are to be slaves; she is Hagar. Now this Hagar is Mount Sinai in Arabia, and corresponds to the present Jerusalem, for she is in slavery with her children. But the Jerusalem above is free; she is our mother. (Gal. 4:22-26)

Though the story of the women is true, their lives also symbolized two covenants: Hagar, the old covenant of law; and Sarah, the new. And this divine allegory gives the entire story greater meaning, for . . .

> as at that time he who was born according to the flesh persecuted him who was born according to the Spirit, so it is now also. But what does the Scripture say? "Cast out the bondwoman and her son, for the son of the bondwoman shall not be an heir with the son of the free woman." So then, brethren, we are not children of a bondwoman, but of the free woman. It was for freedom that Christ set us free; therefore keep standing firm and do not be subject again to a yoke of slavery. (Gal. 4:29—5:1)

"As at that time . . . so it is now also" (4:29). The story gives us eternal truth. Those under the bondage of law have always persecuted those freed purely by grace. As it was with the women's sons, Ishmael and Isaac, so it was with the Pharisees and Jesus, and so it continues in the church today. Nevertheless, " 'Cast out the bondwoman and her son!' " (4:30). Away with legalism and its condemnation! "It was for freedom that Christ set us free; therefore keep standing firm and do not be subject again to a yoke of slavery" (5:1).

Living allegory permeates the entire Bible. And the Holy Spirit helps us to recognize it even as He helped Paul. But the symbolic meaning never negates the truth of the historical account.

The third type of symbolic writing is *prophetic vision*. Prophets often speak to us directly of spiritual reality; and yet attempting to describe the heavenly in terms of earthly things is impossible. So we find in scripture a symbolic "code" used by prophets to describe heavenly things. Consider the vision of the glorified Christ in the first chapter of Revelation.

> And I turned to see the voice that was speaking with me. And having turned I saw seven golden lampstands; and in the middle of the lampstands one like a son of man, clothed in a robe reaching to the feet, and girded across His breast with a golden girdle. And His head and His hair were white like white wool, like snow; and His eyes were like a flame of fire; and His feet were like burnished bronze, when it has been caused to glow in a furnace, and His voice was like the sound of many waters. And in His right hand He held seven stars; and out of His mouth came a sharp two-edged sword; and His face was like the sun shining in its strength. And when I saw Him I fell at His feet as a dead man. (Rev. 1:12-17)

The sight of Him caused a righteous man to fall down as dead. How true! And yet, how far beyond description such a sight must be! I once saw an artist's drawing of Christ as described here. It was grotesque! Far from capturing the glory John saw, it more resembled a gargoyle. And that is because John was writing symbolically, not literally. He was in the Spirit, and what he saw could not be described in earthly terms, for there is nothing on earth like it! And so are all prophetic visions! But God has given the prophets a language of symbols.

A few of the most basic and consistent symbols are used in this description. His eyes, for example, are described as "a flame of fire." The power of His gaze transcends anything ever known on earth; and that power is to purify, and its intensity comes from His jealous love. "Fire" does not describe the physical appearance of His eyes but their power to purify. The use of fire as a symbol of purification is common in scripture.[5]

"Out of His mouth came a sharp two-edged sword." A sword symbolizes the word of God repeatedly in scripture, and represents its authority and irresistible power to accomplish that for which God sent it.

> For the word of God is living and active and sharper than any two-edged sword, and piercing as far as the division of soul and spirit, of both joints and marrow, and able to judge the thoughts and intentions of the heart. And there is no creature hidden from His sight, but all things are open and laid bare to the eyes of Him with whom we have to do. (Heb. 4:12-13)

> And take the helmet of salvation, and the sword of the Spirit, which is the word of God. (Eph. 6:17)

"And His feet were like burnished bronze, when it has been caused to glow in a furnace." Bronze normally symbolizes judgment, and here likely foreshadows the day of vengeance when "He treads the wine press of the fierce wrath of God, the Almighty" (Rev. 19:15; see also Isa. 63:1-6).

This language of symbols is not limited to the books of prophecy, however. It is found richly wherever prophets speak—in the Law, the Prophets and the poetry of scripture especially. And it is important that we are aware of the prophets' symbolic code. But we must not be impatient to decipher it all, or we will make presumptuous errors. For God may not even have revealed the whole as of yet. But as He does, will we be the ones prepared to hear His voice? "Surely the Lord God does nothing unless He reveals His secret counsel to His servants the prophets" (Amos 3:7). As God unveils His secrets in the last days, deceiving spirits also will abound. Are we yet spiritually capable of recognizing false interpretations? "To the law and to the testimony!

If they do not speak according to this word, it is because they have no dawn" (Isa. 8:20). Our necessary preparation, therefore, is to become intimate with scripture and with the God of scripture.

The disciplines of perception and perspective which we have discussed in the last two chapters help us to answer the basic question, "What does is say?" And as we consider the countless answers to this and its family of questions, we must also develop the discipline of testing those answers. For an incorrect answer could be dangerously deceiving. We must not accept any answer as correct until it passes the tests of the second and third principles.

Principle 2

DOES IT HARMONIZE AND FLOW?

Chapter 5

The Blend of Many Voices

The first test we must apply to every scriptural interpretation is the question, "Does it harmonize with the rest of scripture?" In music, harmony is not created by different instruments playing the same note. That only produces unison, and no great symphonies have been written in unison! Harmony is created when the voices play different notes which blend together and move under one baton to synthesize a greater single expression of musical sound.

Likewise, scripture is not a collection of writers who all said the same thing. Their burdens differed, as did their purposes in writing, their perspectives and their personal experiences. And yet the different voices blend to produce a unified expression of the ways of God with man, and man with God.

This harmony serves as an excellent test for all biblical interpretation. But the test cannot be applied casually. Responsible Bible expositors often refrain from teaching or even discussing a new interpretation for six months to a year in order to thoroughly check it against the rest of scripture, both in spirit and in letter. It takes time to expose a teaching to all possible angles of scrutiny. But this is necessary, for if an actual contradiction exists on any level, the teaching is invalid.

A certain amount of familiarity with scripture is necessary in order to use this test in our daily reading. It is therefore wise to begin the study of scripture simply by reading it open-mindedly. I would suggest starting with the New Testament and reading it through—*several times*! It is important to become familiar with its message, its structure, and its natural emphases before engaging in centuries-old doctrinal disputes. Once we have broken the ground of familiarity, we can cultivate an intuitive use of this test to supplement rigorous study: "Does the interpretation agree both in spirit and in letter with the message of scripture *as it would be understood by an objective reader*?"

The test of harmony provides more than a true or false evaluation; it also teaches us degrees of emphasis. Admittedly, there is a sense in which truth is truth and allows for no variation of degree. But there is also great practical wisdom in emphasizing what the Bible emphasizes. Jesus sternly rebuked the Pharisees for tithing " 'mint and dill and cummin,' " while neglecting " 'the weightier provisions of the law: justice and mercy and faithfulness.' "[1] They were correct in the minor matters, but very wrong in allowing them to overwhelm the major ones.

The most important teachings of scripture are commonly called doctrines. They meet three general requirements:

1) Doctrines are expressly taught (not merely implied) at least twice.

2) They are in complete agreement with the rest of scripture, both in spirit and in letter.

3) In matters of practice, such as baptism, the practice is clearly demonstrated.

Teachings which do not meet the first and third requirements for doctrine are not therefore false. But repetition in scripture is not accidental, either, and we must honor the divine emphasis. Special weight must also be placed on teachings which stem directly from divine purpose or divine character *as revealed.* For example, the revealed character of God gives enormous weight to this admonition:

> Beloved, let us love one another, for love is from God; and every one who loves is born of God and knows God. The one who does not love does not know God, for God is love. (1 John 4:7-8)

And the revealed purpose of God in "instruction" must focus all our teaching:

> But the goal of our instruction is love from a pure heart and a good conscience and a sincere faith. (1 Tim. 1:5)

If we lose this focus, we have undoubtedly begun majoring in minors as did the Pharisees, for the Bible's emphasis is consistent with its purpose.

The ultimate plumb line of scripture which places all teaching into perspective is given by Christ when He isolated a single commandment and called it the first and the greatest:

> "Teacher, which is the great commandment in the Law?" And He said to him, " 'You shall love the Lord your God with all your heart, and with all your soul, and with all your mind.' This is the great and foremost commandment." (Matt. 22:36-38)

Our failure to teach *and practice* this commandment is surely our gravest failure in understanding and believing the Bible. Even the tendency to emphasize loving one another above the foremost commandment dangerously undermines true Christian faith and leans toward humanism.

In many ways the harmony within scripture serves as a tool to test our understanding of scripture, both in truth and in significance. Where an interpretation does not harmonize with the whole of scripture, it cannot be trusted; and where our emphasis is not God's, it is out of balance. In the Bible, we see divine emphasis in repetition and expressed priorities, and in revelation of divine character and purpose.

But the harmony of scripture extends beyond itself, for

biblical truth is set in *reality*—both spiritual and natural reality. It is not a revelation suited only to ivory tower philosophers; it works in daily life. If it did not, it would fail in its divinely appointed mission: guiding our lives.[2] But for it to succeed, we must honor *all three* principles of Bible interpretation.

A crucial link between biblical revelation and daily life is the fact that natural reality is temporal, whereas spiritual reality is eternal. Natural reality is also a sin-darkened expression of spiritual reality, whereas biblical revelation is a clear expression of truth which helps us perceive correctly both the natural and the spiritual. If biblical interpretation is separated from daily living, it is no longer harmonizing with God's expressed purpose for the Bible. But if we compromise biblical teaching to agree with worldly thought, we are walking in darkness.

Biblical revelation harmonizes completely with all physical and natural truth. It is human thought, darkened by sin, which fails to understand truth and resists the biblical revelation. Therefore, our understanding of natural reality must be shaped by biblical revelation, and not vice versa. Where human thought says that feelings of guilt are caused by oppressive social values, the Bible says concerning guilt "that they [who do not know the Law of God] show the work of the Law written on their hearts, their conscience bearing witness, and their thoughts alternately accusing or else defending them."[3] Where human thought says that man can preserve society by technological achievement, the Bible says that "unless those days had been cut short, no life would have been saved; but for the sake of the elect those days shall be cut short."[4] And society will be preserved only by the supernatural intervention of Christ's return and the establishment of His government upon the earth. In all such cases we must acknowledge the supremacy of the divine revelation over human thought. And wherever the harmony between scripture and secular thinking seems strained, we must rely upon the Bible.

But what about the instances where harmony within scripture is tense? Here the harmony of scripture serves as more than a test; it becomes a tool for profitable study. For where the Bible appears to us to contradict itself, that is a sure sign that our understanding needs to be sharpened in that particular area. And it is almost invariably beneficial to directly pursue the apparent disharmony until its root is uncovered.

The only exception to this would be where the conflict is trivial, such as an omission in a genealogy. Although enormous energies could be spent in pursuing such matters, the Bible speaks directly to this tendency, saying, "Shun foolish controversies and genealogies and strife and disputes about the Law; for they are unprofitable and worthless."[5] And this agrees with the somewhat colloquial maxim, "Make much of what the Bible makes much of, and little of what the Bible makes little of."

An apparent contradiction may not only expose but also pinpoint a critical area of our scriptural understanding which is out of balance. For example, John 7:24 often stops a young believer short: "Do not judge according to appearance, but judge with righteous judgment" (John 7:24). The verse commands us to judge, and yet elsewhere we are told, "Do not judge lest you be judged yourselves. For in the way you judge, you will be judged; and by your standard of measure, it shall be measured to you."[6] With the emphasis of scripture on judging, we might initially get the impression that all judging is wrong. In that case, John 7:24 would appear as a contradiction. If, however, we use this as a cue to study judging carefully, we will be greatly benefited.

Such a study reveals the difference between condemning judgment and constructive judgment, divinely appointed judgment and presumptuous judgment, righteous judgment and false judgment, eternal judgment and temporal judgment. It will also reveal the instances where we must judge, and the strict boundaries we must observe as we practice this delicate but vital responsibility.

Often, an apparent lack of harmony is deliberate and intended to challenge our thinking. "The proverbs of Solomon. . . . To understand a proverb, and the interpretation; the words of the wise, and their dark sayings" (Prov. 1:1, 6, KJV). A "dark saying" is literally a puzzle, but perhaps is better described as a mystery. And wise men have long used mysteries, as they had used parables, to reveal truth. But, unlike a parable which needs interpretation, a "mystery" is simply a presentation of fact containing a glaring paradox or dilemma. Jesus cites one from the Psalms to expose the spiritual blindness of some Pharisees.

> Now while the Pharisees were gathered together, Jesus asked them a question, saying, "What do you think about the Christ, whose son is He?" They said to Him, "The son of David." He said to them, "Then how does David in the Spirit call Him 'Lord,' saying, 'The Lord said to my Lord, "Sit at My right hand, until I put Thine enemies beneath Thy feet" '? If David then calls Him 'Lord,' how is He his son?" (Matthew 22:41-45)

Such "dark sayings" often reveal the profoundest truths of scripture. In music also, the tensest harmonies often lead directly to the climax of a composition. Therefore, seeming contradictions, especially when given in close proximity without a hint of apology, are a *strong* clue to us that there is sacred treasure near.

For example, the book of Job is one divine mystery. It is not an allegory; it is simply a story. And yet the facts face us with piercing questions, the pivotal one being, "If God promises blessing to the righteous, then why does He let them suffer?" But buried deep in the mystery of Job lies the priceless revelation of how we must respond to God's sovereignty!

God seems to contain the greatest revelations in the vial of divine mystery. How can God become man and still be

God? How can we be in heaven while on earth, or dead while alive? How can God be both merciful and vengeful? How can two people become one in marriage? And the list continues.

Harmony is not lacking in the "mystery." But its very tension promises a profound resolution. Therefore, whenever you see a paradox stressed in scripture, be sure that treasure lies nearby!

Chapter 6

From One Note to the Next

There is a continuity in scripture very similar to the flow in music. Each book of the Bible is like a single movement within a musical masterpiece. Each movement relates to the others and yet contributes something vital of its own to the whole. And within each there is that coherence of motion and singleness of expression which marks the work of a master composer—never a wasted phrase or a pointless digression, every note contributes.

The flow within each book of scripture is equally pronounced, for it carries the burden of the heart of its author. And there is an interflow uniting the many books of scripture, for the same breath of God touched each man who wrote, giving them a common heavenly vision to bear on their differing circumstances. As we discover the flow within each book, we also find the burden from God which compelled the man to write. And there is where we also find the secrets of God's heart revealed. For the intimacy which the authors shared with God and the supernatural nature of the Bible itself combine to show us God's heart on every page. Again there are no wasted phrases or pointless digressions. Every word contributes.

This marvelous flow does not lie on the surface, but *it always appears in the conflict within the hearts of the characters involved.* (Of which you are one. Remember, each command or invitation in the Bible which applies to you makes you a participant in its drama by your response—or lack of response.)

Understanding the concept of flow in scripture, and in all good writing for that matter, we recognize a basic law of hermeneutics, *the law of context.* Essentially it teaches us that the exact meaning of any passage or word can only be determined by its context. For example, how do we determine the meaning of the word "eye"? We cannot always assume the first definition listed in a dictionary. Only the context can tell us if it is a noun or a verb, if it is figurative or literal. (Is it the eye of a radio telescope, a prophet, a hurricane?)

In the same way that the context determines the meaning of a word, it also determines the meaning of a phrase or passage. Where alternative meanings are possible, we must always give the writer credit for intending the meaning which is logically consistent with the context.

Also characteristic of biblical "flow" is clear *purpose.* We must assume that when an author finished a book of scripture, he had succeeded in expressing a particular burden. His purpose for writing was accomplished, and we should be able to recognize specifically what his burden was and how he expressed it. If we do not, that should be the goal of our further study of that book. For only when we perceive the author's burden unfolding do we truly understand the purpose of the book.

As we focus on the author's purpose and burden, we will also see *direction* in the writing. The author starts by establishing common ground with the reader and proceeds from there to his goal, the communication of his burden. Flow will always have *direction.* Follow it! It is your guide to understanding the difficult passages. If correctly understood, it will faithfully unite every thought in the book.

Another dimension of flow is *structure*. Although it varies from book to book in the Bible, there will always be structure; the flow of thought is never random. The simplest type of structure we see in books of the Bible is the *logical argument*. It may be a teaching or an exhortation within a book, or it may be an entire book, such as Deuteronomy or some of the epistles. Usually the direction is clear; the author may even directly state his purpose in the first few verses and then frequently make reference to it as he develops his argument. It may conclude with a summary, a restatement or an exhortation based upon the points proved.

In the historical narratives of scripture, many biblical themes are developed by another structural device, the *cause and effect* relationship. Most often, the person himself experiences the consequences of his actions. But we sometimes see incredibly far-reaching consequences for the actions of biblical characters. Many generations can be affected, either for good or for evil, by the actions or prayers of one person. And as this principle acts in history, we can learn with the perfect vision of hindsight the significance of faith, love for God, obedience, repentance, stubbornness, carelessness, sin, and so on.

A composite of the cause-and-effect motif is the *conflict and resolution*. Here many principles and themes often act together in the demonstration of genuine life struggles. For example, in David's conflict with his son Absalom, we see David reaping judgment from God for his sin against Uriah, we see an undisciplined and neglected son rebelling against society and his father, we see Absalom committing the sins which will lead to his eventual destruction, and we see God sifting the people of Israel by the measure of their loyalty to David. And in the resolution of the conflict, we see God's covenant with David enduring, we see the fruit of David's repentance, and we see the strength of the flesh giving way to the strength of faith. Still more could be added to these lists, but what we must recognize is that a *conflict and resolution* in a historical narrative probably contains many cause-and-effect relationships demonstrating as many different biblical principles. And that of course is true to life.

Throughout scripture we see yet another structural mode, *line upon line.* Biblical themes are developed in this way by reinforcing and by counterbalancing. The book of Proverbs is an obvious example of this type of structure, but it can be observed everywhere in the Bible.

At first, such a passage may not appear to flow at all, but be merely a series of teachings. The story line which contains them may flow, but on the other hand, it too may appear to be a series of unrelated episodes. But the flow always lies in the careful development of the biblical themes, and it is normally found at the level of the heart's conflict.

A simple illustration of this is in the latter part of Luke 10.

> And behold, a certain lawyer stood up and put Him to the test, saying, "Teacher, what shall I do to inherit eternal life?" And He said to him, "What is written in the Law? How does it read to you?" And he answered and said, "You shall love the Lord your God with all your heart, and with all your soul, and with all your strength, and with all your mind; and your neighbor as yourself." And He said to him, "You have answered correctly; do this, and you will live." But wishing to justify himself, he said to Jesus, "And who is my neighbor?" Jesus replied and said, "A certain man was going down from Jerusalem to Jericho; and he fell among robbers, and they stripped him and beat him, and went off leaving him half dead. And by chance a certain priest was going down that road, and when he saw him, he passed by on the other side. And likewise a Levite also, when he came to the place and saw him, passed by on the other side. But a certain Samaritan, who was on a journey, came upon him; and when he saw him, he felt compassion, and came to him, and bandaged up his wounds, pouring oil and wine on them; and he put him on his own beast,

and brought him to an inn, and took care of him. And on the next day he took out two denarii and gave them to the innkeeper and said, 'Take care of him; and whatever more you spend, when I return, I will repay you.' Which of these three do you think proved to be a neighbor to the man who fell into the robber's hands?" And he said, "The one who showed mercy toward him." And Jesus said to him, "Go and do the same."

Now as they were traveling along, He entered a certain village; and a woman named Martha welcomed Him into her home. And she had a sister called Mary, who moreover was listening to the Lord's word, seated at His feet. But Martha was distracted with all her preparations; and she came up to Him, and said, "Lord, do You not care that my sister has left me to do all the serving alone? Then tell her to help me." But the Lord answered and said to her, "Martha, Martha, you are worried and bothered about so many things; but only a few things are necessary, really only one, for Mary has chosen the good part, which shall not be taken away from her." (Luke 10:25-42)

Initially we see an expert in the Law of Moses testing Jesus. And when the two foremost commandments were established, he oddly enough ignored the first, and then showed only a superficial interest in the second. Christ answered his loophole question about the second by admonishing him to have compassion so that he can recognize his neighbor. But what about the first commandment? The lawyer ignored it; did the Holy Spirit also? By no means! Verses 38-42 which may seem to be unrelated are actually the finishing touches provided by the Spirit of God where the foremost commandment is given its place. Verse 42 indeed crowns the passage by emphasizing that only *one* thing is indispensable, sitting at the Lord's feet, listening to His word. Martha and the lawyer had both stumbled in this.

The parable of the good Samaritan is much more complete when the story of Mary and Martha is included. But even as they together teach us the two foremost commandments, they also place in perspective the commission to evangelize as given earlier in the chapter (evangelizing without obeying these commands can be disastrous), and lay the foundation for purity in prayer as taught in the following verses. Outwardly the four passages are unrelated, but in the lessons they teach they are inseparable in the flow of the Gospel of Luke.

Line upon line, or story after story, the lessons of scripture reinforce and counterbalance one another as the biblical themes unfold. This structural device gives unity and flow to what might otherwise appear to be a disjointed narrative. Observing this structure requires much more than a superficial analysis of what we read; it requires a deep and personal exploration of the story's conflict. But we have two faithful guides from the Holy Spirit to ensure that our exploration is both secure and profitable—the activity in the hearts of the biblical characters involved, and the marvelous flow of harmonious biblical themes which always mark the proper course. How much like music is scripture!

The flow of scripture—its purpose, direction and structure—is found most clearly when a book is studied as a whole. Most of the books represent the work of a single author and therefore give us the burden of God through the eyes and the heart, the life and the sufferings, of one godly man. Usually, the content of a book is united by a single burden on the heart of its author; to discover that burden is to find the key to understanding God's purpose for that book. (And *the flow* will show it to you.) Often, God gave the burden of His own heart directly to the man who wrote, as He did with Hosea in a dramatic way. And the burden of God's heart, that which compelled each book to be written, *is* the lifeblood of scripture. And nothing gets us closer to it than the burden on the heart of the writer! Once we discover it, we have begun to tread holy ground; we stand on the threshold of all the blessing that God can give through those chapters—wisdom, faith, the fear of God—for out of God's heart pour all His mercies. And in wisdom we are wealthy beyond gold, in faith we receive all grace, and in the fear of God we become intimate with the Holy One.[1]

Friend, do not be content with a superficial reading of the Bible. Immerse yourself in it. Find the flesh and blood of the patriarchs, weep with the prophets, tremble and pray with David, and be prepared to meet the heart of God.

Principle 3

DO I HARMONIZE AND FLOW?

Chapter 7

This Music Not Written for Computers

The late Dr. Howard Hanson, composer of the lovely "Romantic Symphony," said, "If you want to write music with computers, then let the computers play it and all the other computers sit around and enjoy it. I have no interest in that sort of thing." Dr. Hanson knew that music apart from the compassions and dreams of the human heart is empty. And because that living element can never be programmed into a computer, a computer can never learn to appreciate great music. That may be a humorous thought, but instructive: we also cannot appreciate music apart from our own heart's response.

As you continue your study of the Bible, it is my hope that you will discover it to be a coherent flowing revelation of God and His ways among men—the timeless Treasure that has sustained the Faithful for thousands of years. But what if you don't? What if after much study its message still seems jumbled and irrelevant, with God portrayed as less than faithful or too distant to love? As in music, so with the Bible—*knowledge* can carry a person only so far! The mind can understand and play notes, but *only the heart can sing.*

61

When training a musician, it is necessary to thoroughly teach harmony, rhythm, phrasing and form. But a musician is not born out of these things. They are only his tools, as hermeneutics and inductive study are a Bible student's tools. There comes a time when he must be challenged to "respond" personally and intimately to the music as he hears it coming from his own instrument and as he anticipates the next notes to play. Only as he does this can he "shape" his tone and his phrasing to recreate in his audience, and in himself, the feelings of the composer. This is the true joy of performing music. And there is scarcely a person alive who cannot enjoy good music when performed well, even if he knows nothing of music theory or happens to be tone-deaf! But if the musician plays only notes and does not allow his emotions to be totally captivated and carried, he will never spark passion or rouse mystery in his listeners, because music is an experience—*heart to heart*.

And so with the Bible. Unless you respond personally and intimately to what you read, you will find very little meaning or beauty in it. In music, the composer allows us to "touch" his heart and experience some of his feelings. Through scripture, God allows us a far more profound experience of "touching" *His* heart, and receiving new life like a breath from heaven. But without personal response, neither music nor the Bible can "come alive." Communication that is merely intellectual does not require a response to be understood, but like music, the Bible is not primarily intellectual communication. And our understanding is all too often limited by our response.

We understand much of the Bible by faith.[1] In other words, where the mind either cannot prove or cannot comprehend a matter, we submit our understanding to God and ask Him to inscribe the truth in our spirits and hearts instead. And then as we respond personally to the scripture, we receive understanding from God's Spirit directly into our own spirits. The mind is *involved*, but faith is not primarily an intellectual experience. *Faith is RESPOND-ING from our innermost self—our hearts and our spirits—to the truth of God's Word.* A merely intellectual approach to the Bible can never unlock its depths or potential.

Our first two principles of Bible study are like tools, and very reliable ones. But it is possible to know them and use them, and still not discover the richness of scripture, because they are primarily intellectual tools. The crucial principle is really the third one—our response.

"Do I harmonize and flow?"

"Does my life harmonize with God's Word? And am I flowing with God's Spirit, with His will for my life, and with His people?" This is what gives insight into the scriptures!

The apostle Paul explains the principle this way:

> For who among men knows the thoughts of a man except the spirit of the man, which is in him? Even so the thoughts of God no one knows except the Spirit of God.
>
> Now we have received, not the spirit of the world, but the Spirit who is from God, that we might know the things freely given to us by God, which things we also speak, not in words taught by human wisdom, but in those taught by the Spirit, combining spiritual thoughts with spiritual words. But a natural man does not accept the things of the Spirit of God; for they are foolishness to him, and he cannot understand them, because they are spiritually appraised. But he who is spiritual appraises all things, yet he himself is appraised by no man. For who has known the mind of the Lord, that he should instruct him? But we have the mind of Christ. (1 Cor. 2:11-16)

Here Paul distinguishes between the "natural man" who does not accept the things of the Spirit of God, and the "spiritual" man who "appraises" (discerns) all things. And by this he refers to the words he speaks which are taught by the Spirit of God rather than by human wisdom. The natural man's problem is not with Paul, but with "the things of the Spirit of God," which must include all scripture, since "All Scripture is inspired by God."[2] If anyone finds the Bible impossible to understand or accept, this could therefore be the reason: "A natural man does not accept the things of the Spirit of God; for they are foolishness to him, and he cannot understand them, because they are spiritually appraised" (1 Cor. 2:14).

We must, of course, understand what Paul means by natural and spiritual. A study of the context of the passage, and a related passage (Gal. 5:19-26), indicates that Paul is not distinguishing between Christians and non-Christians. In fact, in the next three verses, Paul rebukes that very church for being "fleshly" and "walking like mere men."

> And I, brethren, could not speak to you as to spiritual men, but as to men of flesh, as to babes in Christ. I gave you milk to drink, not solid food; for you were not yet able to receive it. Indeed, even now you are not yet able, for you are still fleshly. For since there is jealousy and strife among you, are you not fleshly, and are you not walking like mere men? (1 Cor. 3:1-3)

What Paul means by spirituality is the degree to which a person's heart and life have been transformed by God, and the extent to which his will is yielded to God—in other words, *how much he harmonizes and flows with God!* This is a direct factor in his ability to understand scripture, and the essence of our third principle.

We can discover the Bible to be an inexhaustible treasure of wisdom and revelation, and a source of joy and strength, where each new insight clarifies our vision of God, His kingdom, and our place in His eternal plan. But this happens only as we take each insight and apply it directly to our individual lives and hearts to bring *ourselves* into harmony *with God's Word.* Only in this context of living faith does God's Word come alive by the Spirit of God to transform hearts and heal broken lives; only in this context of living faith can it reveal eternal truths, and usher us into the eternal blessings of God the Father.

A seed may show none of its life until it is planted in

good soil. And in the same way the scriptures show little of their potential apart from a heart of faith. Jesus used that very illustration in the parable of the Sower where He describes the ideal soil as "an honest and good heart."[3]

Jesus expresses this principle in yet another way in John 7:17, "If any man is willing to do His will, he shall know of the teaching, whether it is of God. . . ."

A basic law of hermeneutics warns us against taking a passage of scripture out of its context in the Bible. But the *gravest* distortions of scripture result from taking the whole Bible out of its intended context of "an honest and good heart," and putting it into the harsh environment of a bitter or wicked heart.

God's intended context for the Bible must never be forgotten:

> "But prove yourselves *doers* of the word, and not merely hearers who delude themselves." (James—James 1:22)

> "Therefore everyone who hears these words of Mine, and *acts* upon them, may be compared to a wise man, . . . And everyone who hears these words of Mine, and does not act upon them, will be like a foolish man, who built his house upon the sand." (Jesus—Matt. 7:24, 26)

> "The secret things belong to the LORD our God, but the things revealed belong to us and to our sons forever, that we may *observe* all the words of this law." (Moses—Deut. 29:29)

God has always intended the Bible as a guide for living, and as a source of encouragement and strength for those who desire to remain faithful in difficult times. God gave the Bible to men and women who had a covenant, or agreement, with Him to trust, love, and obey Him that He in turn might take care of them, bless them, and glorify His name in their midst. And He gave each portion of scripture to them *to help them walk in that covenant, or restore them to it if they had broken it,* so that He could continue to bless them and establish His name in the earth![4] Apart from such a covenant, the Bible is "out of context" and may well be misinterpreted, distorted or even rejected as false.

Observe how dramatic an effect this "covenant relationship" has on a person's ability to understand the Bible by considering one illustration. Suppose a "natural man" endeavors to understand the righteousness of God. As he studies the Bible, he will observe God's commandments, Israel's obedience and disobedience, and the gross disobedience of most Gentile nations. And then he will observe God sending prophets to warn the people, God sending judgments of famine, disease and military overthrow, and God occasionally relenting of His judgment—for no apparent reason other than one person's persuasive argument, or somebody sprinting through the camp with an incense burner, or some other such incidental event. The final result of his study may depict God's righteousness as a bizarre array of slaughter and unexplainable leniency related to Israel's observance of some rather peculiar laws. He may also find the Bible clear on the ordinances, but be left wondering why God would ever care so much about a day of the week that someone should be stoned to death for working on it; or why it would make such a big difference to Him if one offered a pig on the altar instead of a lamb; or why all of these laws were seemingly thrown to the wind after Jesus Christ came.

Now suppose, on the other hand, that someone undertook this study with a desire to follow God's commands and harmonize with His righteous standards. Assuming he was clear as to the covenant of his day and that he was sincerely trying to live in accordance with that covenant, he would quickly discover a powerful force *within his own heart* that resisted and opposed his efforts to be true to that covenant. (See Romans, chapter 7, for details.) And he would soon realize that his own heart defied the righteousness of God and could never live up to it. The experience is painful and directly assaults his pride and self-reliance. But, at this point, the "seed," the word of God, begins to germinate. If he has "an honest and good heart,"[5] he desires to persevere in righteousness even though he knows that his heart loves sin. So he lets his pride break, and says, "God, I can't do it. Please help!" That whole experience is called repentance, and the "seed" begins to take deep root.

Now all this time, God has been watching and even helping to bring this person to his present crisis. And if He left him there, he would remain helpless and frustrated. But God's covenant is workable; He *knows* the weakness of the human heart.[6] And He has been waiting to give this person some "good news." He may or may not have heard it before, but now his *heart* is ready to receive it! And so whether he recalls the "word," reads it, or hears it, the Spirit of God now helps him understand and believe. The "word," the "good news" from God, is this: "I know you can't do it—by yourself. But I have made a way for you. I have taken your sin, and you now *are* righteous in My eyes because of your faith. Only listen carefully to My voice, and continue to walk humbly with your God."[7]

Righteousness becomes his by *faith* as the Spirit of God helps him to *personally enter* into that eternal covenant; the "seed" can now grow to maturity. (NOTE: Certain aspects of the covenant *have changed*[8] over the centuries as Israel's history has unfolded, but *the requirements of the heart* have always been the same. We are to love Him with our whole heart, trust Him as a loving Father to take care of us in a hostile world, believe Him, and obey His voice.[9] He in turn will provide for us and guide us; He will satisfy our hearts with good things; and He will glorify His name in us as His Spirit empowers us. The actual experience of entering into this covenant always involves receiving perfect righteousness by faith,[10] since God is holy and cannot be intimate with corruption. From that point we grow; and obedience becomes easy[11] as we learn to love God and trust Him by getting to *know* Him.)

Now, how does his understanding of God's righteousness compare with the "natural" man's? They have both read the same Bible, but the natural man sees God as harsh, inconsistent and petty; whereas the one in covenant with God has brought new personal experience to bear on his understanding. By applying the scriptures to his own life, he has learned first of all how impossible it is for anyone to be righteous before God in his own strength. But he has also learned that God's provision for man's sinfulness is *more* than adequate if he will come in faith to receive what God has provided. And because he has tasted the free gift of God's righteousness, he now understands a mystery called "the beauty of holiness."[12] And this allows him to appreciate the intense longing in God's heart to see His people living in holiness.[13] Now as he reads the records of God's dealings with Israel, he can share the grief of God's heart caused by sin. He could not do that before. And he knows by experience the beauty of God's gift that Israel spurned by their sin. He can rejoice when any true standard of righteousness or intercession is raised that allows God to withhold judgment, and he can even share the pain in God's heart when He ultimately has to judge sin in order to cleanse the land. Because of his living faith, he has touched *the heart of God* and now has a genuine basis for understanding the scriptures. And without a doubt, his ability to sense God's heart is his surest resource for *illuminating* the scriptures.

Even "peculiar" ordinances begin to make sense. It becomes clear to him that God was vitally concerned about the Sabbath because it typified[14] a basic element of the covenant—the fact that man can do nothing in his own strength to escape from the power of sin and death, and therefore must *rest with faith* in what God has done.[15] And it even becomes clear, under the present covenant especially, why God wanted only certain animals to be offered on His altar—not because He had particular tastes in meat, of course! But once again, it typified an element of His covenant—God's provision for our sin and for our weakness. God's provision is perfect. He did not want blemished or unclean animals sacrificed on His altar because it would distort the image of what God was doing by providing His Son as the perfect sacrifice—taking our sin by the shedding of His blood, the blood of the covenant, and giving us spiritual, eternal life by the offering of His flesh.[16]

We see therefore that a person in covenant with God has the only adequate basis for understanding the Bible, especially since the dawn of the new covenant when many mysteries of scripture were fulfilled in Jesus Christ,[17] and when new intimacy with God's heart was made possible by the cross and by the outpouring of the Holy Spirit. Attempting to understand the Bible apart from such a covenant is taking the Bible as a whole out of its intended context, and is like trying to understand a seed without ever planting it in good soil!

"Do I harmonize and flow?"

This principle can be of benefit in two different ways. First, it can direct us to the proper personal foundation for understanding scripture and receiving eternal life.[18] And second, it can help us recognize doctrinal error by understanding its cause. This second aspect of the principle will be discussed in chapter nine. But first, let's examine our personal foundations.

Chapter 8

Getting in Tune

I have often enjoyed listening to the radio program that takes a "safari through the Bible in five years." But as we prepare to consider our personal foundations for faith and scripture understanding, we will be taking a "short stroll through the Bible in about five minutes."

Although this quick survey cannot provide the detail of a five-year study, it is well suited for refreshing our perspectives. And healthy perspectives are vitamins to those who desire to grow in their knowledge of God (theology) and in their relationship with Him (faith). Perhaps these next five minutes will trigger a growth spurt in your spiritual life.

It all begins with God revealing himself to man. The first way He did this—in life and in the Bible—is as Creator. When Adam and Eve considered God, they knew Him as their only companion; they had no earthly parents or siblings. They knew Him as personal, intelligent and unfathomably powerful, yet One with whom they could talk as a friend. We can only imagine the harmony that filled their earthly paradise, for they were as close to God as to one another. Yet when they sinned, they ran from Him and hid.

It is interesting that no one had to tell them to hide from

God. Although they had no previous knowledge of evil, they knew that their Creator would be their judge—"Hath not the potter power over the clay?" (Rom. 9:21, KJV). For just by knowing God as Creator, Adam and Eve knew Him well. Besides understanding His power, His intelligence and His authority over all He made, they also knew the beauty of His heart, reflected in their paradise and the joy they once had walking with Him in the garden.

But then God called to them, "Where are you?"[1] and they tasted for the first time the redeeming love of God. He was reaching out to them, His heart grieved by their sin and loss but already intent upon restoring to them all they had lost—and more! God reaching out to fallen man is the theme which fills the rest of scripture. Redemption!

The combined revelation of God as Creator and Redeemer forms our complete understanding of His nature, His works and His purposes. As Creator, we see Him as eternal, holy, powerful and self-existent—a Person, a Judge, a King. As Redeemer, we see God reaching down out of His eternity and His holiness to help stumbling mankind. He atones for their sin and works to reestablish fellowship with them. He pours out His Holy Spirit to strengthen, heal, guide, and glorify them. He calls them by name, and ultimately joins to himself all believers for an eternity of adventure, beauty and fulfillment tantamount to the unspeakable glory of God himself—heaven.

God's redemptive acts reveal more about His nature— His mercy, His sacrificial love, His desire to reach down to the humble, and His ability to purify and exalt them. And as Redeemer He shows us His unique concern for mankind whom He created in His image and redeems to His image.

One of God's first redemptive acts for fallen man was to bar the way to the tree of life lest man should eat of it and live forever in a fallen condition, thus permitting man's physical death.[2] And He then guarded the tree with cherubim for the day when man could eat of it and live forever sharing God's holiness.[3] It may seem strange that death is one of God's redemptive provisions for us. But God saw that mankind needed to be purified as well as redeemed, and in His wisdom He ordained that purified life should spring forth out of death—a true redemptive provision.[4]

Not only is our physical death redemptive, but God centered His work of redemption in the death of His Son on the cross. And Jesus calls us to join Him in that death and resurrection, promising us that it is our only path to true life. (In Romans, chapters five and six, Paul theologically underscores this truth.)

> "Truly, truly, I say to you, unless a grain of wheat falls into the earth and dies, it remains by itself alone; but if it dies, it bears much fruit." (John 12:24)

> Then Jesus said to His disciples, "If anyone wishes to come after Me, let him deny himself, and take up his cross, and follow Me. For whoever wishes to save his life shall lose it; but whoever loses his life for My sake shall find it. For what will a man be profited, if he gains the whole world, and forfeits his soul? Or what will a man give in exchange for his soul?" (Matt. 16:24-26)

We see from the structure of the Bible that God's work of redemption is its main *activity*. In the third chapter, the way to the tree of life is barred (Gen. 3:22-24), and in the final chapter, it is restored to "those who wash their robes" (Rev. 22:14), those who receive God's redemptive work on their behalf. Very little is revealed about the glories of heaven, although some have had a glimpse, such as Paul and John (who were not even allowed to repeat certain things that they heard!).[5] But near the end of the Bible, God evidently picks up where He left off in paradise with unfallen man, now with redeemed and eternally purified man, to resume with him the adventure of His delight.

The scope of the Bible, therefore, and man's short life on earth as we know it, is God's testing, purifying, and redeeming work, with only certain basic and critical truths revealed about the "hereafter," such as the certainty of judgment and rewards, including heaven and hell. But the little that is revealed about heaven, coupled with the revelation of God's creative and loving nature, assures us that it will be more desirable than the human heart can comprehend, and that perceiving this with eyes of faith is a step of true wisdom. Likewise, what little is revealed about hell is sufficient to warn us that though many go there, it is not the more tolerable for it, and that there is nothing to be dreaded more. For the redeemed, any thought of the hereafter should teem with excitement and hope, like a bride's anticipation of her wedding. For so it truly is![6]

By revealing himself as Creator and Redeemer, God is also declaring the core of our relationship to Him—*we are His,* because He created us.[7] He is free to do with us as He pleases. And because He is a God of love, He has chosen to fill our lives with good things, to satisfy us with "honey from the rock,"[8] and to feed us with the "finest of the wheat" if we will love Him and walk humbly before Him.

But we have rebelled and chosen to walk independently of Him, in our own plans, our own desires, and our own strength. "There is a way which seems right to a man, but its end is the way of death."[9] And God in turn paid the price to redeem us from the slavery of sin and death into which we have sold ourselves. And so once again, we belong to Him. "You are not your own. For you have been bought with a price."[10] "You were not redeemed with perishable things like silver or gold from your futile way of life inherited from your forefathers, but with precious blood, as of a lamb unblemished and spotless, the blood of Christ."[11]

Obviously, then, those who walk as if they owe no account and can freely be their own masters are not walking *in harmony* with the revelation of the Bible on this point. "For we shall all," including Christians, "stand before the judgment seat of God" (Rom. 14:10). And to personally *harmonize and flow* with this, we need to acknowledge God's rights over us as Creator and Redeemer, seek to understand His desires concerning us and His purposes for us, and then live to please Him. Our rewards will be from God himself; *all* the good that He desires to do for us, now and for eternity, will be ours. And there is no one who knows as well as God how to satisfy the desires of the human heart; after all, He made it!

And for those who choose not to walk before God as Creator and Redeemer, but to make their own way, by their own standards and their own strength, God will allow them to continue and eventually eat the bitter fruit of their ways and their corruption.[12] And their judgment will also be eternal.

What are God's desires and purposes for us? From the beginning God has desired to make us objects of His love. He has always desired to fill us with His blessings and to demonstrate His love and His greatness by all that He does for us and through us. But most of all, He wants to share His heart with us and be a companion. God desires that we be intimate with Him, and for that purpose He made us in His image. And He intends that we grow in that relationship for eternity, after the pattern of marriage as we know it, but with heavenly perfection!

But because of God's holiness and righteousness, His desires for us cannot be realized as long as we walk in sin, squandering our affections on the things of this world that will pass away so quickly, instead of loving Him with all our strength.[13]

God desires therefore that we walk in such a way that His love can reach us.[14] But how can we do that? How can we walk worthy of God? Our own flesh and heart will fail us![15]

God has provided a way. "Without faith it is impossible to please Him, for he who comes to God must believe that

He is, and that He is a rewarder of those who seek Him"
(Heb. 11:6). *Faith* is God's provision for us.

> For I am not ashamed of the gospel, for it is the power of
> God for salvation to everyone who believes, to the Jew
> first and also to the Greek. For in it the righteousness of
> God is revealed from faith to faith; as it is written, "But
> the righteous man shall live by faith." (Rom. 1:16-17)

Faith, remember, is *responding* from our innermost
self—our hearts and our spirits—to the truth of God's
Word. And so faith is, *first* of all, yielding personally to the
authority of the Almighty God our Maker and to the lordship of Jesus Christ our Redeemer.

> Therefore also God highly exalted Him, and bestowed on
> Him the name which is above every name, that at the
> name of Jesus every knee should bow, of those who are in
> heaven, and on earth, and under the earth, and that every
> tongue should confess that Jesus Christ is Lord, to the
> glory of God the Father. (Phil. 2:9-11).

Since God has revealed to us His desire concerning the
lordship of His Son Jesus, the response of faith is confessing
with our tongues that Jesus Christ is Lord, and submitting
to His authority.

> "The word is near you, in your mouth and in your
> heart"—that is, the word of faith which we are preaching,
> *that if you confess with your mouth Jesus as Lord*, and be-
> lieve in your heart that God raised Him from the dead, you
> shall be saved; for with the heart man believes, resulting in
> righteousness, and with the mouth he confesses, resulting
> in salvation. For the Scripture says, "Whoever believes in
> Him will not be disappointed." For . . . "Whoever will call
> upon the name of the Lord will be saved." (Rom. 10:8-13)

The word of faith is, "that if you confess with your
mouth Jesus *as Lord*, and believe in your heart that God
raised Him from the dead, you shall be saved." As we personally yield to the lordship of Christ by faith, and trust
God's work of redemption on our behalf, we experience
what the Bible terms "new birth." In new birth we actually

receive new life from heaven, and are called new crea-
tures.[16] And this life is not mortal, but eternal. . .

> for you have been born again not of seed which is perish-
> able but imperishable, that is, through the living and
> abiding word of God. For, "all flesh is like grass, and all its
> glory like the flower of grass. The grass withers, and the
> flower falls off, but the word of the Lord abides forever."
> And this is the word which was preached to you. (1 Pet.
> 1:23-25)

New birth results from an act of faith on the part of an
individual. But as the term "birth" rightly implies, it is
only the beginning of a "life" of faith. For then *relationship*
with God begins, along with the joy of knowing *Him*.

As we enter into relationship with God by new birth, we
discover Him to be our *friend*! "The *Lord* is for me; I will
not fear; What can man do to me?" (Ps. 118:). "If God is for
us, who is against us?" (Rom. 8:31). "While we were yet
sinners, Christ died for us" (Rom. 5:8).

If you have ever felt that God is against you, those feelings certainly did not result from faith. Could He who gave
His life for the forgiveness of our sins possibly be our enemy? We have a different enemy, Satan; but God is for us!
And as we walk in faith, we are constantly encouraged by
the fact that the all-powerful God is on our side! He first
delivered us from sin and death by the death and resurrection of Christ; and as we encounter all of life's problems, we
know that the mighty God is at work in us. He is even our
Advocate if we sin.[17] It is His desire "to do good for us,"[18]
and He does, as we walk in faith—responding personally
and intimately to the truth of God's Word. The privilege of
having God as a friend gives great encouragement!

We also begin to know God as a *companion*.

> "Behold, the virgin shall be with child, and shall bear a
> Son, and they shall call His name Immanuel," which
> translated means, "God with us." (Matt. 1:23)

> "I am with you always, even to the end of the age." (Matt.
> 28:20)

There is a way in which God is everywhere and we could not escape from Him if we tried,[19] but that is not companionship. There is another way in which we can experience and enjoy the presence of God in a personal way. This is, of course, a subjective type of experience, and hard to define and describe in a way that would be meaningful to everyone. But "God with us" is a treasure that nevertheless is unique to the Christian and cannot be minimized. Companionship with God changes the very nature of living! We are never alone, Someone always understands, Someone is always there to comfort or give wisdom—Someone who loves us perfectly. No aspect of life is untouched with His presence. Nothing remains empty or lifeless.

The best illustration I know of for what *companionship* with Jesus does is the first miracle that He performed on earth. It is a miracle that many Christians experience in life—Jesus turning water into wine at the wedding. When we enter into covenant *with Him*, a richness enters into our daily life that wasn't there before simply because we are sharing it with Him. A simple pleasure becomes a gift from a Friend, and He's there to thank. Even the most mundane matter somehow is touched with eternal significance only because Jesus is with us, sharing the moment. He has changed water into wine! How can one explain companionship to one who has not known it? It *must* be experienced! "What we have seen and heard we proclaim to you also, that you also may have fellowship with us; and indeed our fellowship is with the Father, and with His Son Jesus Christ" (1 John 1:3).

And thirdly, we can know God as our *Father*:

"Pray, then, in this way: 'Our Father who art in heaven,'. . . Look at the birds of the air, that they do not sow, neither do they reap, nor gather into barns, and yet your heavenly Father feeds them. Are you not worth much more than they?. . . Do not be anxious then, saying, 'What shall we eat?' or 'What shall we drink?' or 'With what shall we clothe ourselves?' For all these things the Gentiles eagerly seek; for your heavenly Father knows that you need all

these things. But seek first His kingdom, and His righteousness; and all these things shall be added to you."
(Matt. 6:9, 26, 31-33)

Jesus admonishes us to remember that having a heavenly Father makes a difference. We do not have to be anxious;
we do not have to live like those who have no heavenly
Father and who must "eagerly seek" their own provision.
We can seek first His kingdom and His righteousness, and
know that God will care for us.

Having God as a Father means, "I belong." It means, "I
am not one insect among billions, but I am honored and
cared for by the Almighty; I am a son, I am a daughter. I
shall inherit glory one day, and indeed my heavenly citizen-
ship is already recorded."[20] It also means, "I am one with
all others whose Father is God; we are one family."[21] And it
means, "This earth is not my home; I am only sojourning
here for a time. And while I am here, my heavenly Father is
taking *good* care of me!"[22]

Relationship—friend, companion, Father. "God is *for*
me, God is *with* me, I *belong*." God intends for us to share
intimacy with Him in all these ways and more. And as we
do, that relationship quickly becomes more precious than
physical life. "Thy lovingkindness is *better* than life" (Ps.
63:3).

It seems that many Christians sell themselves short of
their high calling to know God, and prefer instead the worries of the world, the deceitfulness of riches, and the desires
for other things.[23] But this will change as God purifies His
Church in the days which remain before Christ's return.
And so to them I say. . .

> "Let us know, let us press on *to know the LORD.* His going
> forth is as certain as the dawn; and He will come to us like
> the rain, like the spring rain watering the earth." (Hos.
> 6:3)

And. . .

> Let us also lay aside every encumbrance, and the sin which
> so easily entangles us, and let us run with endurance the
> race that is set before us, fixing our eyes on Jesus, the
> author and perfecter of faith, who for the joy set before
> Him endured the cross, despising the shame, and has sat
> down at the right hand of the throne of God. (Heb. 12:1-2)

And to those who have never tasted the joy of knowing
God, I say. . .

> If you confess with your mouth Jesus as Lord, and believe
> in your heart that God raised Him from the dead, you shall
> be saved; for with the heart man believes, resulting in
> righteousness, and with the mouth he confesses, resulting
> in salvation. . . . "Whoever will call upon the name of the
> Lord will be saved." (Rom. 10:9-10, 13)

Therefore, call upon God! Trust His redeeming work on
your behalf. Confess with your mouth Jesus as Lord of all,
and Lord of your own life in particular—your desires, your
affections, your actions, your thoughts.

> And the Spirit and the bride say, "Come." And let the one
> who hears say, "Come." And let the one who is thirsty
> come; let the one who wishes take the water of life without
> cost. (Rev. 22:17)

Salvation and relationship with God are freely available
to anyone and everyone. The choice is yours now. The
choice will not be yours forever, though; only the *consequences* of your choice will be yours forever. Therefore,
choose Jesus as Lord and Saviour, and live faithfully to that
choice.

These are the foundations that God has given us in the
Bible. They are our foundations for knowing *about* God,
and for knowing God; they are our foundations for life itself,
and of course for understanding scripture.

Once we lay in our lives the foundation of salvation and
commitment to Christ, the Bible becomes more than a book
to us. Much more. It becomes our milk, our food. "Like
newborn babes, long for the pure milk of the word, that by it

you may grow in respect to salvation, if you have tasted the kindness of the Lord" (1 Pet. 2:2-3). And we then have the necessary foundation for personally understanding the Bible. With our minds we can draw upon our own experience of walking by faith[24] to help us understand what we read. With our hearts, we can identify with the struggles and temptations of men and women whom God is calling into covenant with himself, and we can empathize with God's heart as He guides and purifies His people. And with our spirits we learn to "hear" the voice of our Shepherd.

> "The sheep hear his voice, and he calls his own sheep by name, and leads them out. When he puts forth all his own, he goes before them, and the sheep follow him because they know his voice. And a stranger they simply will not follow, but will flee from him, because they do not know the voice of strangers." (John 10:3-5)

As we learn to read the Bible prayerfully, we hear our Shepherd calling us by name and beckoning us to follow. Though our earthly names are not written in scripture, we still somehow sense God singling us out and calling us individually to follow and obey Him. Through scripture, and the Gospels especially, we learn to recognize the tender voice of our God who sacrificed His life for us, as "the good shepherd lays down His life for the sheep" (John 10:11). And as we face temptations and conflicts in the world, we learn to discern the voices of strangers that beckon us to follow a thief or a robber. And with our spirits we also learn to "see" beyond the conflicts in life and in the Bible to the consistent purposes of God in restoring us to His image and the image of His Son.

Enormous revelation is contained in the Bible which the natural mind cannot perceive. To unlock the depths of scripture, the *life* of faith is necessary, of which becoming a Christian is only the first step. All too many Christians fall under Paul's rebuke in 1 Corinthians 3:1-3 for being fleshly. Thus the question . . .

"Do I harmonize and flow?"

Chapter 9

On Playing with Broken Strings

There is one more vital benefit that we can receive from the third principle: we can use it as a tool to recognize and understand doctrinal error!

If we are careful to apply this principle to our own study of scripture, it will keep us on stable ground. But like a two-edged sword, it works equally well when swung in the other direction! We can apply the principle to the bearers of every teaching or doctrine. Do they have their own interests in mind, or God's?

> Jesus therefore answered them, and said, "My teaching is not Mine, but His who sent Me. If any man is willing to do His will, he shall know of the teaching, whether it is of God, or whether I speak from Myself. He who speaks from himself seeks his own glory; but He who is seeking the glory of the one who sent Him, He is true, and there is no unrighteousness in Him." (John 7:16-18)

A man who seeks God's glory and desires to do His will can bring true doctrine; but a man who speaks from himself with impure motives distorts the truth, whether he does it deliberately or not. And since all doctrine comes through *people*, the purity of all doctrine is vitally affected by the condition of the person's heart who brings it! And we can best understand an error or deception by understanding the sin that causes it.

For example, Paul explains the doctrine of the "false circumcision," or legalizers, as an effort to escape persecution for the cross of Christ, and a desire to boast in the flesh of others (Gal. 6:12-13). Paul does not say that it was a deliberate attempt to deceive. But he still pinpoints a sin behind their deception. And it is easy to understand the zeal of the legalizers when you recognize how strong their desire was to escape persecution and to boast! Paul simply saw their sinful motive, and recognized it as the root cause of their doctrinal error.

Jesus also identifies the doctrine of the Pharisees as a fruit of sin in their hearts.

> And He said to them, "Rightly did Isaiah prophesy of you hypocrites, as it is written, 'This people honors Me with their lips, but their heart is far away from Me. But in vain do they worship Me, teaching as doctrines the precepts of men.' " (Mark 7:6-7)

Considering these examples a bit further, we can see why it takes more than hermeneutics to keep doctrines pure! Indeed, experience sadly teaches us that a person will jump from one deception to another with unabated zeal if he is corrected exegetically while his heart is allowed to continue in its sin.

It seems that for every biblical truth, there are at least a half dozen different ways to distort, deny or nullify it. And to catalogue all doctrinal error, heresy, and cult theology would be a mammoth task,[1] while keeping it current would be impossible! But the sins of the heart today are the same as they have always been or ever will be. "There is nothing new under the sun" (Eccles. 1:9).

It has been observed that the best way to recognize counterfeit currency is to know the real thing intimately, and this is true for doctrine also. But studying heresies can be very valuable if we search for the consistent sins which spawned them, since heresies, like weeds, can be best controlled by attacking their roots!

We will all be confronted with questionable doctrines at times, and we need a consistent biblical basis for evaluating them. But besides Bible study, that foundation must include a sensitivity to sin acquired through personal purity and experience. "First take the log out of your own eye, and then you will see clearly enough to take the speck out of your brother's eye" (Matt. 7:5).

There are some common sins among those who zealously embrace or promote false doctrine, and we will consider ten of them. The first five are overt sins against scripture, and they can often be detected directly in the arguments for a particular doctrine. The last five are sins of the heart, and they create the weakness in the individual for deception. The sins of the heart may be harder to pinpoint, but a direct sin against scripture is a clue to us that there is a deeper problem. This list is not necessarily exhaustive, but it should give us a feel for what we are dealing with.

1. Rejecting any portion of true scripture (blatant or tacit). Conversely, adding to scripture.

This serious sin against scripture is committed by many cults blatantly and by some Christians in subtle ways. And yet, scripture expressly warns us against it.

> "You shall not add to the word which I am commanding you, nor take away from it, that you may keep the commandments of the Lord your God which I command you." (Deut. 4:2)

> "Whatever I command you, you shall be careful to do; you shall not add to nor take away from it." (Deut. 12:32)

> Every word of God is tested; He is a shield to those who take refuge in Him. Do not add to His words lest He reprove you, and you be proved a liar. (Prov. 30:5-6)

> I testify to everyone who hears the words of the prophecy of

this book: if anyone adds to them, God shall add to him the plagues which are written in this book; and if anyone takes away from the words of the book of this prophecy, God shall take away his part from the tree of life and from the holy city, which are written in this book. (Rev. 22:18-19)

The first two passages refer to Moses' commandments, the third to "every word of God," and the fourth to the book of Revelation. But quite clearly, God does not want us to misrepresent Him by tampering with any part of His Word. And we see from the following two passages just how much He desires us to respect His Word.

(Moses speaking) "And you said, 'Behold, the Lord our God has shown us His glory and His greatness, and we have heard His voice from the midst of the fire; we have seen today that God speaks with man, yet he lives. Now then why should we die? For this great fire will consume us; if we hear the voice of the Lord our God any longer, then we shall die. For who is there of all flesh, who has heard the voice of the living God speaking from the midst of the fire, as we have, and lived? Go near and hear all that the Lord our God says; then speak to us all that the Lord our God will speak to you, and we will hear and do it.'

"And the Lord heard the voice of your words when you spoke to me, and the Lord said to me, 'I have heard the voice of the words of this people which they have spoken to you. They have done well in all that they have spoken. Oh that they had such a heart in them, that they would fear Me, and keep all My commandments always, that it may be well with them and with their sons forever!' " (Deut. 5:24-29)

"For My hand made all these things, thus all these things came into being," declares the Lord. "But to this one I will look, to him who is humble and contrite of spirit, and who trembles at My word." (Isa. 66:2)

Certainly God does not want us to alter His Word!

We have the rich heritage of the true Canon of Scripture, the Bible, which we recognize as the authoritative Word of God. And we have many true scholars faithfully transmitting those texts to us in our language. These sixty-six books were not collected and affirmed on a subjective basis, but on a historical one, in an effort to preserve the message which was confirmed by signs and miracles in demonstration of the authority of God, such as it was through Moses, the prophets, Jesus and the apostles. Their contemporaries sometimes did participate in the actual writing, as did Ezra, Luke and Mark, but the authority of the message itself stemmed from the profound demonstrations of God's own power. And these writings assembled together, the sixty-six books of the Bible, recount for us God's work of redemption for mankind from beginning to end. Hence, the Cannon is complete. We accept those particular books today because historically the people of God, i.e., the Jews and early Christians, considered those writings to be the true message of God confirmed by the power of God; and as such, they stand alone. Furthermore, we recognize that other writings, both historical and inspirational, may be true, but that the Canon cannot be added to because as the account of God's redemptive work, it is complete. And we recognize that it is the standard against which all other revelation must be weighed, both in spirit and in letter.

It is beyond the scope of this chapter to go into extensive detail on the historical development of the Canon, or the thousands of ancient manuscripts which support its authenticity, or the many modern archaeological discoveries which continue to confirm its accuracy. But the treasure is ours to revere as the authoritative word of God. And it is the basis for all doctrine.

With the excellent translations and study tools available today, it is not difficult for anyone to understand basic doctrine if he will read with an open mind and heart. But one sure way to undermine correct doctrine is to attack the Bible itself by rejecting any portion of it, or adding to it. Tragically, efforts are made to do both.

The reason that this does so much to subvert doctrine is

that it upsets the exquisite *balance* of scripture. The Bible typically presents a truth by developing it through the life experiences of several different people, which exposes all sides of an issue in an entirely non-cosmetic fashion. But when one side is omitted, the image of truth is distorted, even without altering the other passages which are considered. Heresy itself has sometimes been described as "truth out of balance," and in some cases, that is true. One could argue strongly for a false doctrine merely by presenting one side of the issue and then demanding a decision based on only that part of the evidence. "The first to plead his case seems just, until another comes and examines him" (Prov. 18:17).

Four ways of rejecting portions of scripture have become quite common simply because we have not recognized them for what they are. But they are sin, even though cloaked in piety or apparent scholarship.

The first is *tacit rejection*. Here a person abuses the scriptures by deliberately ignoring the portions he doesn't like. It may not appear to be an attack on scripture at all, since the rejected portions are not outwardly criticized. But if his *motive* is to create a biased impression of what the Bible says, it is just as damaging. (Notice please that the mere omission of passages while teaching cannot be construed as sin. It is so *only* if the omissions are designed to deceive.)

The second way to reject portions of scripture is *inconsistent treatment*. For example, if certain historical accounts are taken literally while others are taken figuratively, we have inconsistent treatment. It is easy to see how someone who wanted to slant a teaching could use this device effectively. For instance, if he wanted to present Christ as a good moral teacher only, he could say that the teachings of Christ literally happened, while the miracles of Christ were only a figurative expression of how much his teaching helped people feel better and become better people. An objective eye would insist that the manuscripts give no reason for treating the passages so differently, and that whether or not one believes it, there can be no doubt that the Bible declares such miracles to have taken place. To say that the Bible teaches otherwise is nothing less than rejecting a portion of scripture.

A third way is *incorrect dispensationalizing*. Dispensations refer to the periods of time marked by a progression of covenants which have governed mankind's relationship to God, and Israel's in particular. Since the covenants have changed, certain aspects of the relationship have also changed. For example, Christians are not obligated to the ceremonial laws of Moses as the Jews once were. But the teachings of the Bible can be distorted by inventing dispensations which the Bible does not teach, or by claiming that the character of God has changed as the covenants have changed. An illustration of the former would be to claim that the Church entered into a new dispensation after the Canon of scripture was completed and affirmed. That being true, we would have reason to expect differences in our relationship to God from what the early church experienced. However, the objective eye once again insists that the Bible teaches no such new covenant or dispensation, and that we today can expect the same type of relationship with God that the Church in the first century enjoyed. To teach otherwise is to reject, in a subtle way, the Bible's teaching on the nature of Christian experience.

The fourth way, the most tragic, is *blatant rejection*. Have you ever heard statements like these? "The book of James is just not as inspired as Romans." "The first eleven chapters of Genesis are only poetry." "Anyone who thinks that God is dealing with him like He dealt with Job is just full of pride!" In all three instances, the statements are direct efforts to remove those portions of scripture from consideration in matters of doctrine. In other words, it's okay to read them as long as we don't take them too seriously. Usually, when statements such as those are made, the circumstances make it plain enough what particular teachings are being "shielded" from the truth of those scriptures.

An equally dangerous sin is that of *adding to scripture*. This is not done with hymnals, catechisms or study guides. But to consider writings to be of equal authority with the Bible and of equal significance in determining doctrine is pernicious. Many cults employ this technique to support their beliefs, such as Christian Science with *Science and Health with Key to the Scriptures,*[2] and Mormonism with *Book of Mormon, Doctrine and Covenants,* and *The Pearl of Great Price.*[3]

A related masterpiece of devilry is to accept the Bible as inspired, but to use a "corrected" version. The Jehovah's Witnesses and Mormons both have their own private versions. The reason, quite simply, is that all accepted translations refute their theology. They each needed a new "translation" in order to maintain their doctrines and still claim to accept the Bible. *The New World Translations*, as used by the Jehovah's Witnesses, contain seemingly minor alterations (such as substituting "a god" for "God" in John 1:1) and were prepared under the guise of scholarship.[4] The Mormon version of the Bible, on the other hand, is more liberal with its "corrections" and does not claim scholarship as its source, but rather "direct revelation from God."[5] In contrast, Christian Science does not have its own private version, but merely its own private interpretation as given by Mary Baker Eddy in *Science and Health with Key to the Scriptures,* which they consider to be equally inspired.[6]

Although we cannot delve into the whole maze of cultism here, these three samples should underscore the fact that just because a religion claims to accept the Bible as inspired and authoritative doesn't necessarily mean that its teachings are based upon the true Canon of scripture and upon it alone.

All sound doctrine must reflect the balance of scripture as revealed through its teaching and the life experiences of its characters. And to reject any portions from consideration in doctrine, by any method, can seriously distort the true message of the Bible.

2. Pitting one scripture against another.

Once again, the balance of scripture is targeted. And it is done by claiming that the counterbalancing scriptures actually contradict each other, giving us the option of either throwing them both out as if they were offsetting votes in an election, or taking our pick of which one we choose to believe. This approach can never lead to correct understanding of the Bible, because its premise is that the Bible contradicts itself, which it does not. If a person claims that two portions of scripture contradict each other, it merely demonstrates that he does not fully understand either one. We must recognize the harmony of the two before we can confidently declare their meaning.

For example, a simple way to attack the doctrine of the Trinity would be to claim that a verse like Deuteronomy 6:4, which emphasizes God's oneness, *contradicts* passages like Daniel 7:9-14 or Acts 10:38, which emphasize God's distinct person. Since the correct understanding derives from the harmony of passages such as these, placing them in opposition to one another is an effective way to create confusion. And out of that confusion, any number of bastard doctrines may arise.

To pit any scripture *against* another will cause doctrinal confusion. Proper understanding always comes from discovering the harmony of passages such as these, through *consistency* in applying the simple principles of hermeneutics.

3. Seeking support for preconceived ideas— closed-mindedness.

In order to understand the problem with this approach,

we must remember that the purpose of Bible study is to discover what the Bible says, not to make the Bible say what we want it to. The problem, therefore, is not one of violating a particular principle of hermeneutics, but of losing objectivity! And in so doing we are predisposed to slant whatever we read and to bend or break any number of rules, perhaps even unknowingly!

We all have opinions and some measure of preconceived ideas which affect the way we perceive things. That is to be expected, and that is why objectivity in Bible study is as difficult as objectivity in news reporting. But it is necessary for honesty!

We need to continually remind ourselves to ask, "What does it say?" and not, "How can I find support for this particular idea?"

4. Endeavoring to reconcile God's truth with worldly philosophy—compromise.

This is actually a specific variety of the previous sin, but an especially prevalent one. Paul gives us stern warning against this in Colossians 2:8, "See to it that no one takes you captive through philosophy and empty deception, according to the tradition of men, according to the elementary principles of the world, rather than according to Christ." And again in 1 Corinthians 1:20-21, "Has not God made foolish the wisdom of the world? For since in the wisdom of God the world through its wisdom did not come to know God, God was well pleased through the foolishness of the message preached to save those who believe."

The wisdom of the world is so far inferior to the wisdom of God in the gospel message that it is foolishness by comparison. And perversely enough, the gospel message appears foolish to those whom the world considers wise. Never the twain shall meet! Endeavoring to reconcile the two runs the risk of seriously compromising God's truth as revealed in the Bible.

A difficulty we sometimes encounter in understanding the gospel is that we have been so inundated with the world's philosophies that we do not recognize them for what they are. In that condition the only way we can understand God's truth is to clearly spell out the world's philosophies side-by-side with the teachings of the Bible until we recognize the pivotal differences. The two are often found to be in direct opposition.

For example, situation ethics stems from the philosophy that there are no moral absolutes—that not only is everything relative, but that everything is also changing. Here is the pivotal difference. The Bible insists that true morality reflects God's perfect and changeless character, giving us a perfect and changeless standard; and therefore its moral teachings will always stand in sharp contrast to the concept of situation ethics. They can never be reconciled.

Perhaps the most subtle and dangerous philosophy is secular humanism. In actuality it is more than a philosophy; it is a religion—in creed, in faith, in propagation and in worship. And yet, we hardly recognize it as either; it seems to masquerade blithely as some new-found virtue! Consider the differences. Humanism, under three twentieth-century manifestos, calls us to serve mankind, declaring that serving an invisible God is meaningless. It calls us to render all our talents for the betterment of mankind, declaring that devoting our talents to God is a waste of mankind's resources. It calls us to a new morality which measures all questions by the benefit accrued to society, declaring that Judeo-Christian morals are repressive and destructive to happiness. And it calls us to *save* society by our education and technology, declaring that all other avenues are a delusion.

The Bible teaches an entirely different religion, insisting through Christ that " 'you shall worship the Lord your God and serve Him only' " (Luke 4:8). And it compels us to render all our talents as a living sacrifice to God, for He alone is worthy. It declares God's moral standards as eternal and calls us to be holy, for God is holy. And it promises that God will set world affairs in order at the second coming of Christ.

God is concerned about mankind, as He demonstrated in the compassionate ministry of Jesus Christ. But we, like Jesus, are called to serve God, and to minister to the needs of mankind only as He directs. God is concerned about our happiness, but He knows that pleasure from sin is short-lived, and that true joy only comes with surrender of everything to the lordship of Christ. And God is concerned about the problems in the world, but He knows that in order for the world to be filled with peace, plenty and brotherly love, it too must first be subjected to the lordship of Christ. And alternative routes to the betterment of mankind, personal happiness or world peace are delusions.

Secular humanism and Christianity are therefore antithetical on all basic points of faith and practice. They cannot be reconciled, for they worship different gods. And we must be careful to uphold these differences without compromise.

5. Accepting (or rejecting) teaching without personal study and prayer—carelessness.

Sometimes a teaching just "sounds so good" that we are tempted to believe it without investigating for ourselves. Perhaps we heard it from someone we admire, or maybe we just grew up with the idea. But this carelessness is a widespread problem among Christians. For example, I can't recall how many times I've heard that the Bible says, "God helps those who help themselves." Have you ever tried to find that verse? (While you're looking, ponder Matthew 6:31-33.)

Now these were more noble-minded than those in Thessalonica, for they received the word with great eagerness, examining the Scriptures daily, to see whether these things were so. Many of them therefore believed . . . (Acts 17:11-12)

Be diligent ["study," KJV] to present yourself approved to God as a workman who does not need to be ashamed, handling accurately the word of truth. (2 Tim. 2:15)

As mentioned earlier, the first five sins that we have been considering can often be observed directly in a doctrine or teaching, for they all relate in some way to the first two principles of interpretation, "What does it say?" and, "Does it harmonize and flow?" But abusing the scriptures in any of the above ways suggests a deeper sin—one that can be detected only in the persons themselves, in those who started the doctrine in question and also in those who perpetuate it.

The next five sins, then, may not appear directly related to doctrine. But we must remember Paul's explanation of our third principle:

But a natural man does not accept the things of the Spirit of God; for they are foolishness to him, and he cannot understand them, because they are spiritually appraised. (1 Cor. 2:14)

To the pure, all things are pure; but to those who are defiled and unbelieving, nothing is pure, but both their mind and their conscience are defiled. They profess to know God, but by their deeds they deny Him, being detestable and disobedient, and worthless for any good deed. (Titus 1:15-16)

An impure heart will distort doctrine. And the sins of the heart that we are about to consider have been the seedbed for many widespread heresies and errors. Neither the Bible nor history teach an exact correlation which links every particular heresy with a particular sin, but the general correlation is strongly established in both. And we need to understand the consequences of a devious heart to matters of doctrine. This understanding will teach us to evaluate all questionable teaching by examining its source as well as its substance; it will make us sensitive to doctrinal weakness in individuals even before tragic deception sets in; it will guide ministers to recognize and challenge the root cause as well as the doctrinal error itself;[7] and it will compel us to examine our own hearts whenever doctrinal questions arise.

6. Refusing to yield to the guidance or conviction of the Holy Spirit.

The Bible shows us that those who consistently disregard God's guidance or commands gradually lose their ability to receive His guidance and understand His commands. Paul and Jesus both described such people with these words of Isaiah:

> "For the heart of this people has become dull, and with their ears they scarcely hear, and they have closed their eyes; lest they should see with their eyes, and hear with their ears, and understand with their heart and return, and I should heal them." (Acts 28:27; Matt. 13:15)

With their consciences seared so badly, they cannot bring pure doctrine. In fact, Paul warns us that they bring doctrines of demons!

> But the Spirit explicitly says that in later times some will fall away from the faith, paying attention to deceitful spirits and doctrines of demons, by means of the hypocrisy of liars seared in their own conscience as with a branding iron, men who forbid marriage and advocate abstaining from foods, which God has created to be gratefully shared in by those who believe and know the truth. (1 Tim. 4:1-3)

On the other hand, we also know that those who consistently obey become sensitive to God's Spirit so that they can discern good from evil and also understand the deeper concepts of scripture—the "solid food" mentioned here (and also in 1 Corinthians 3:2):

> Concerning him we have much to say, and it is hard to explain, since you have become dull of hearing. For though by this time you ought to be teachers, you have need again for someone to teach you the elementary principles of the

oracles of God, and you have come to need milk and not solid food. For everyone who partakes only of milk is not accustomed to the word of righteousness, for he is a babe. But solid food is for the mature, who because of practice have their senses trained to discern good and evil. (Heb. 5:11-14)

By obedience our spiritual senses become trained, and by disobedience they become dull to the point where we cannot understand the "meat" of scripture. Our spiritual diet is then limited to milk, like a baby's.

Therefore, if we desire to probe the depths of scripture, we must grow in obedience, taking each revelation from scripture and applying it to our lives as honestly as we can. As we do this, our understanding will grow. But to disregard the counsel of the Spirit of God and refuse the lordship of Christ is to injure our spiritual senses and thereby destroy our foundation for understanding the Bible.

7. Lust for knowledge.

Knowledge makes arrogant, but love edifies. If anyone supposes that he knows anything, he has not yet known as he ought to know; but if anyone loves God, he is known by Him. (1 Cor. 8:1-3)

Throughout scripture, and perhaps most emphatically in Proverbs, knowledge is extolled as a treasure. But its value can only be realized within the context of a greater treasure, love. It is true wisdom to understand that "if I have . . . all knowledge . . . but do not have love, I am nothing" (1 Cor. 13:2). And a desire for knowledge without the humble desire to walk in love can only foster pride. It becomes a destructive lust incapable of edifying anyone. "Knowledge makes arrogant, but love edifies" (1 Cor. 8:1).

The Gospel is simple,[8] and pure doctrine reflects that. "But the goal of our instruction is love from a pure heart and a good conscience and a sincere faith" (1 Tim. 1:5). This declaration of Paul's to the young pastor is echoed throughout the books of Timothy and Titus. In those books, often called the pastoral epistles, Paul makes it very clear that the purpose of teaching and exhortation is to encourage godly living and faith with pure attitudes so that the gospel of Christ may be lived and proclaimed without bringing reproach to the name of God. And yet, many people desert this purpose and spend their energies on useless arguments which disrupt faith.

> But the goal of our instruction is love from a pure heart and a good conscience and a sincere faith. For some men, straying from these things, have turned aside to fruitless discussion, wanting to be teachers of the Law, even though they do not understand either what they are saying or the matter about which they make confident assertions. (1 Tim. 1:5-7)

> Let all who are under the yoke as slaves [employees] regard their own masters as worthy of all honor so that the name of God and our doctrine may not be spoken against. And let those who have believers as their masters not be disrespectful to them because they are brethren, but let them serve them all the more, because those who partake of the benefit are believers and beloved. Teach and preach these principles. (1 Tim. 6:1-2; see also vv. 3-5)

> This is a trustworthy statement; and concerning these things I want you to speak confidently, so that those who have believed God may be careful to engage in good deeds. These things are good and profitable for men. But shun foolish controversies and genealogies and strife and disputes about the Law; for they are unprofitable and worthless. (Titus 3:8-9; see also Titus 2:3-10)

These exhortations consistently remind us that "knowledge makes arrogant, but love edifies." Nowhere is this truth more tragically demonstrated than in doctrinal strife between churches. Sound doctrine must be maintained,[9] but some denominations appear to be built entirely upon a concept of doctrinal supremacy, a higher revelation. The unity of such churches is founded in pride, not in love. And only love is the perfect bond of unity.[10] Such churches often concentrate their "evangelism" upon other church-goers, and do so by arguing doctrine rather than by sharing the gospel. Endeavoring to sow seeds of discontent rather than seeds of life, they appeal to a person's pride rather than to his need for God's grace. Such an approach is often successful because many church-goers are discontent. But it is a deceitful remedy to meet that discontent with knowledge which only makes arrogant. Contentment comes only through living truth, a personal closeness with God gained through true brokenness and humility, not through more knowledge with pride.

The desire to walk in love and obedience to God brings a hunger for wisdom, wisdom for godly living and faith. But to study scripture with a lust for knowledge and the pride of superior revelation is to invite deception.

8. Idolatry.

> For the time will come when they will not endure sound doctrine; but wanting to have their ears tickled, they will accumulate for themselves teachers in accordance to their own desires. . . . (2 Tim. 4:3)

If our own desires are not in a godly perspective, we once again extend an open invitation to deception where hermenuetics alone cannot rescue us. Misplaced affections are perhaps the gravest problem in Christendom today, for they are in essence idolatry.

God gave us the first commandment, " 'You shall have no other gods before Me' " (Ex. 20:3). And to violate that law is idolatry. Christ crystallized this when He declared that the great and foremost commandment in the Law is, " ' "You shall love the Lord your God with all your heart, and with all your soul, and with all your mind" ' " (Matt. 22:36-38). To violate this law is spiritual adultery, the root of idolatry.

The doctrinal distortions that stem from misplaced affections are horrendous, and limited only by Satan's

imagination. For if we do not obey the foremost commandment, how can we obey the others?

> O sons of men, how long will my honor become a reproach?
> How long will you love what is worthless and aim at decep-
> tion? (Ps. 4:2)

> "Do not lay up for yourselves treasure upon earth, where
> moth and rust destroy, and where thieves break in and
> steal. But lay up for yourselves treasure in heaven, where
> neither moth nor rust destroys, and where thieves do not
> break in or steal; for where your treasure is, there will your
> heart be also." (Matt. 6:19-21)

> " . . . and the desires for other things enter in and choke
> the word, and it becomes unfruitful." (Mark 4:19)

What we love, what we trust, whom we believe, where
we store our treasure—these things all speak loudly of
whom or what we worship. If we love pleasure or things or
family *more* than God, it is idolatry. If we trust in money or
technology or science *more* than in God, it is idolatry. If we
believe scientists or philosophers or economists *more* than
God, it is idolatry. If we store our treasure in land or banks
or reputation *more* than in God, it is idolatry. And that particular sin can blind our minds and harden our hearts as
surely as outward disobedience. Idolatry not only undermines our ability to grasp truth, but it also makes our heart
vulnerable to deception, even to the point of zealously em-
bracing a deadly error. The sin is so dangerous to our Christian walk that the apostle John closes his first epistle with
the warning, "Little children, guard yourselves from
idols."[11]

If we choose not to love what God calls us to love, but
rather to let our affections roam as they will, we cut ourselves off from God's chosen avenue of blessing. "Watch
over your heart with all diligence, for from it flow the
springs of life" (Prov. 4:23). The "springs of life" are all the
blessings of God that we receive by faith. Remember, "with
the *heart* man believes" (Rom. 10:10), not with the mind.

And if we poison our heart, we lose our ability to receive the blessings of God by faith. We may continue to understand with our *minds* to some degree, but the blessing of the Scriptures, the life-giving power of the Word of God breathed fresh from heaven, will elude us.

. Do you desire the springs of life? Then watch over your heart with all diligence. "Keep seeking the things above, where Christ is, seated at the right hand of God. Set your mind on the things above, not on the things that are on earth" (Col. 3:1-2).

9. A self-serving faith.

This particular perversion of heart has corrupted much teaching over the years. It might be considered a form of idolatry where self is worshiped, but perhaps more accurately it is an attempt to justify other forms of idolatry. An entire body of thought has been built upon this error, and its appeal stems from its basic message: "You can have all the blessings of the Bible without counting the cost. Find any blessing in scripture and just claim it; all you have to do is believe."

It is not wrong to desire the promised blessings of scripture, nor is it wrong to teach that God desires to give us those blessings. The desires are healthy and the teaching is true. But that's not the whole story! God has a greater desire than just to give us whatever we want; and we must also have a greater desire than just to receive blessing. Scripture warns us about praying selfishly in James 4:3, "You ask and do not receive, because you ask with wrong motives, so that you may spend it on your pleasures." Our greater desire should be to see His kingdom come in righteousness and power.

"But seek first His kingdom, and His righteousness; and all these things shall be added to you." (Matt. 6:33)

"Pray, then, in this way: 'Our Father who art in heaven,

Hallowed be Thy name. Thy kingdom come.'" (Matt. 6:9-10)

The kingdom of God is not brought near by glutting ourselves with everything that our eyes may desire.

God knows our hearts. We may fool others and perhaps even ourselves, but never God. He sees, He knows. We must humble ourselves before God and ask Him to purify our desires. As God purifies our desires, we then can begin to practice godliness with contentment. And there is where we must stay and grow. There is where God will test our hearts and renew them to His image. There is where our hearts begin once again to burn with a desire for Him and His kingdom. And there God, who alone can judge our hearts, can give us the assurance of a pure heart.

But the error of a self-serving faith turns this all around. We need not deal with our hearts. We only need to ask for whatever we want, and God is humbly there to grant all our selfish desire. Man is served by God.

Those who promote this reversal sanctify it by indicating that as we exercise our freedom to have whatever we want, we are to build the kingdom of God. Their exact teaching is that God has done all that He ever will do until Christ's return. It is now entirely up to us. We have the tools, we have the commission; we cannot wait for God, for He does not intend to do anything anyway. And we thereby become sovereign.

But there are two problems with that idea. First, it doesn't seem to work that way; most followers endeavor primarily to gratify their own desires. Second, that isn't the way God intended the kingdom to be built. It is not God's intention to have a million little sovereigns scurrying about the earth building a kingdom. Where we have a million sovereigns, we have a million kingdoms. God wants one kingdom, and He alone is sovereign! To this the book of Job is a powerful witness.

But we see a beautiful thing about God's ways through

this cloud of doctrinal confusion. Where a person's heart is right, where he truly desires to see God's kingdom built, God honors the desires of his heart and uses him in the kingdom work. Even if his understanding falls short, God honors a pure heart! And that is very encouraging to know.

The error of a self-serving faith never would have come into existence, however, had we first obeyed the command to " ' "love the Lord your God with all your heart, and with all your soul, and with all your mind." ' "[13] For God's blessings would have been abundant, and the work of the kingdom would have been progressing powerfully.

Neither would there have been any passivity. Passivity may seem to be the opposite error of wresting sovereignty from God, but it betrays the same sin of heart—failing to love God fervently. How, then, do we balance the two? The answer is so simple it may stun you—*obey from the heart*! If you learn to love the Lord your God with all your heart, you cannot possibly fall short of His high calling! But any substitute will lead to error.

10. Desiring to justify self.

A very common error of heart that leads to error in interpretation is the desire to justify oneself. It is particularly dangerous because if left unchecked it can be totally consuming and leave the sinner absolutely blind to what he is doing. It is a strong tendency of the carnal heart to rationalize its wrong attitudes, and it should not surprise us at all that carnal Christians turn this tendency against scripture. When they do, it takes two forms, *permissiveness* and *legalism*.

The error of *permissiveness* directly accommodates the heart which loves the world and the things of the world. The reason is clear, "the love of the Father is not in him" (1 John 2:15).

But the error of *legalism*, which seems so different, has the same root. The person does not obey from the heart, and he feels the need to justify himself. So he offers to God outward observances which seem very austere as a substitute for inward obedience.

Where is the balance between permissiveness and legalism? Again, the answer is so simple—obey from the heart! But if we do not obey from the heart, we must repent and ask God for help. Attempting rather to justify ourselves will only lead to error.

These last five sins emphasize how vital a pure heart is to pure doctrine, for "with the *heart* man believes."[14] No matter how educated the mind may be, an impure heart will consistently distort truth.

Chapter 10

The Fine Art of Bible Study

When you listen to a concert violinist like Isaac Stern perform Beethoven, what are you hearing? Is it the genius of the composer being poured through a totally passive vessel? Or is it the momentary inspiration of a man in an ethereal state of musical experience?

Most certainly it is neither. What you are hearing is the intense work of an artist, the fruit of enormous concentration and self-control. His sole purpose is to recreate from notes on a page the multi-dimensioned expression of music that poured from the composer's heart. To do this he must adhere to strict rules of musical interpretation, and yet within those confines make intimate personal response to the music.

One thing that has made Isaac Stern so great is that he knows that the beauty of Beethoven comes from Beethoven, not Stern. He only needs to find it and be the living vessel to carry that beauty to others. He must be sensitive and subjective, but also humble and objective. He must put himself into the music, and yet keep himself out of the way. If he is not emotionally consumed by it, the music is stale; but if he takes it over, Beethoven is crowded out. And

Beethoven, not Stern, must be expressed!

That is the art of musical interpretation, and here are the demands:

1) thousands of hours of careful practice spent mastering the technique of the instrument;
2) an understanding of music theory, of musical styles and eras, and of phrasing and other interpretive skills;
3) a well-rounded repertory;
4) a love for good music;
5) the artistic ability to serve—that is, to become personally involved without personally dominating;
6) artistic self-control—that is, the ability to respond subjectively within strict objective limitations.

How similar are Bible interpretation and musical interpretation? How deep does their resemblance go? And in what ways do they differ?

A key to similarity is that neither music nor the Bible can "come alive" without *personal involvement*. On the other hand, one can read a newspaper and receive nearly 100% of its message with only intellectual attention. But music and the Bible both remain essentially lifeless without the interpreter's involvement. This is because they both speak beyond our intellect.

But they are not identical. Music speaks in a *nonverbal* way directly to a person's emotions, and at times even to his spirit. There are no images of people, places, conflict or story; and yet our imaginations often provide images to suit the feelings stirred. There is motion, sometimes flowing, sometimes violent; there is harmony, sometimes knotted, sometimes placid; and there is the mystery of melody, a virtual personality in itself which experiences the motion and harmony. In this nonverbal way, the composer has somehow shown us something of his heart which can be experienced only by momentarily yielding our emotions to the sound.

The Bible speaks in a *verbal* way, filled with images of people and story. But if we read it like we read a newspaper, only to find out what happened once upon a time, it will disappoint us. For the Bible speaks to our spirits, and through scripture God has shown us something of His heart which can be tasted only by permanently yielding our hearts to Him. In the same way that music comes alive only when the performer is responding to it, the beauty of the Bible can be seen only when a person is consumed by its truth. For the beauty of the Bible is the beauty of life, the full glory of life as it was conceived in the heart of God, its source. And the truth of the Bible can be loved only as it is measured by the wondrous life it produces in a broken person who embraces it—and even more so when our broken world embraces it at Christ's return.

Is interpreting the Bible an art form? In a sense it is, for like interpreting music, it involves both the mind and the heart.

The objectives of Bible study are also similar to the artistic objectives of music. In the case of one, it is to take notes from a page and respond to them in such a way that the feelings in the composer's heart can be experienced in your own heart and conveyed to others. In the case of the other, it is to take words from a page and respond to their message in such a way that the burden of God's heart can be experienced in your own and conveyed to others.

And the demands of Bible study are quite similar to the artistic demands of a performing musician.

1. Where the musician needs to spend thousands of hours mastering the technique of his instrument, the interpreter of scripture needs to spend thousands of hours becoming intimate with the content of the Bible (an hour a day becomes a thousand in less than three years).

2. Where the musician needs to learn music theory,

styles, eras, and interpretive skills, the Bible student needs to understand hermeneutics, and to learn about historical background, biblical culture and language.

3. Where the musician needs to develop a broad repertory, the Bible student needs to apply biblical principles to a wide range of life experiences—especially his own!

4. Where the musician must deeply love music, the Bible interpreter must love truth and wisdom. If he does not, he will never discover or convey the richness of scripture.

5. Where the musician needs to be a servant, and become involved without personally dominating, the Bible interpreter must also allow the biblical message to first touch and transform his own heart before he can proclaim that message to others with any depth of significance. And yet, like the musician, he must not discolor its message by the limitations of his own heart. Such stewardship demands deep humility.

6. And finally, where the musician needs artistic self-control, the Bible interpreter also must respond subjectively within the strict objective limits of hermeneutics.

Another similarity is the *growth process* that each must undergo.

One cannot hurry the maturing of a performing artist. It only comes through his years of dedicated daily work. And though he may at some moment along the way be termed an artist, that is a superficial mark. He is an artist because he is growing and will grow until the day he dies. A technician may master his trade, but no artist has ever walked the boundaries of expressible beauty.

That is so true in Bible study. A scholar is a learner; an interpreter is an experiencer. No one has ever sounded the depths of biblical truth or the heights of faith's adventure. God is unsearchable, yet nothing is as rewarding as seeking His face!

It is a growth that can come only with patient, prayerful

study and watchful obedience. This means many hours of study, hours which can be accumulated only by daily effort. Daily reading also allows time between sessions to reflect upon what you read, and it keeps the scriptures always fresh in your mind for your personal growth.

So give it time, and enjoy that time. When a child discovers a new flower or something new he can do with mud, he can be sure that someone has discovered it before. But that doesn't take any of the joy out of it for him! And we also can find great joy in discovering a living truth from God's Word, though a million others may know it already. The formula for that joy is simple: one section at a time, by patient and careful reading. (I am currently studying the Tchaikovsky violin concerto. I have always loved to listen to it, and now as I practice, I am not racing to "finish" my study of it. Rather, line by line and phrase by phrase I am trying to get as much out of the music as possible—and enjoying every minute of it. I may never "finish" studying that concerto!)

Remember to quiz yourself often as you read, to make sure that you know *what it says.* And the more scripture you study, the more chance you will have to see *harmony and flow.* Remember also that the most significant truths will focus on the heart of man and the heart of God, rather than on the circumstances which served to reveal their hearts.

Count each discovery a treasure, and rejoice in it. God took care not to burden us with unimportant matters in the Bible. Each truth of scripture can enrich your life in some way.

Receive each discovery deep in your heart, and unite it with faith[1]—believing in your heart, and obeying from the heart. The true goal of the Bible study, and its greatest challenge, is to see life come from the Word, to see the "seed" grow to maturity. Hermeneutics can bring us to the best possible understanding of what the Bible says, but only faith can release its life-giving power.

And finally, pray for understanding. Bible study is one part of the overall devotional life of the Christian and cannot be divorced from the rest of it. I have often found my deepest insights into scripture in a time of prayerful contemplation. It is, after all, God who gives insight into scripture. Consider this illustration:

> And behold, two of them were going that very day to a village named Emmaus, which was about seven miles from Jerusalem. And they were conversing with each other about all these things which had taken place. And it came about that while they were conversing and discussing, Jesus Himself approached, and began traveling with them. . . . And beginning with Moses and with all the prophets, He explained to them the things concerning Himself in all the Scriptures. . . . And their eyes were opened and they recognized Him; and He vanished from their sight. And they said to one another, "Were not our hearts burning within us while He was speaking to us on the road, while He was explaining the Scriptures to us?" . . . Now He said to them, "These are My words which I spoke to you while I was still with you, that all things which are written about Me in the Law of Moses and the Prophets and the Psalms must be fulfilled." Then He opened their minds to understand the Scriptures, and He said to them, "Thus it is written, that the Christ should suffer and rise again from the dead the third day; and that repentance for forgiveness of sins should be proclaimed in His name to all the nations beginning from Jerusalem. (Luke 24:13-15, 27, 31-32, 44-47)

Though the men were disciples, they could not understand the scriptures until Jesus opened their eyes and opened their minds. There is no better teacher than Christ himself; He makes our hearts burn within us as He reveals to us truth from scripture. But we must walk with Him on the dirt road, and listen to Him as He speaks. We must obey and we must pray. There is still room at His feet for listeners like Mary of Bethany.[2] And there is still a call to those who desire intimacy with God. Our response, our only logical response,[3] is to wholeheartedly offer ourselves to God to obey Him, and to wrest time from our schedules to prayerfully sit before Him and His Word, asking Him to open the scriptures to us and to speak afresh the words which have power to transform lives and hearts.

As you do this, may your heart burn within you also.

SUPPLEMENTS

Supplement A

Some Common Methods of Bible Study

The principles of Bible study will do us little good if we never read the Bible. How, then, do we proceed to study it? Now the value of methods becomes apparent! What follows is a survey of the common methods that shows the particular purpose served by each one. As we understand these purposes, we should be able to structure a personalized Bible study program which utilizes any or all of them according to our needs.

But it is also appropriate to mention that Bible study is not our only Bible reading. Devotional reading is the other dimension of Bible reading which cannot simply be classified as another study method. Our spirits must be kept healthy by worshiping and praying together with David and the other psalmists, and by sitting at Jesus' feet and hearing the admonitions of all scripture. The study methods which involve primarily our minds are indirectly serving a greater purpose, the strengthening of our spirits. For from the mountaintop view of scripture, we see in every direction the call to return to our once-abandoned relationship with God, to return to the still-vacant place at His side that is reserved for us where we can be nurtured and where we can know Him. Bible study is necessary to support our devotional reading, and indeed its primary purpose is to fully equip us for the life of faith and the work of the Kingdom. Therefore let us recognize it not as an end in itself, but as one of the basic elements in the devotional life of the Christian.

Reading Methods*

There are many schedules for reading the Bible through in a year, but these are not actually *study* methods. Their whole purpose is simply to keep us reading; therefore, they are actually reading methods. But they are important, because whatever actual studying we do must be kept in perspective with the whole Bible. And a simple reading method serves that purpose. For the initial survey of scripture that a new believer must undertake, better methods are available. Rather than once through the Bible in a year (approximately fifteen minutes per day intended to supplement other study), I recommend reading the New Testament alone, straight through several times, without trying to "study" it. An hour a day will take us through in twelve days, reading aloud. But it's actually very easy to do in a week with a *modern paraphrase* for three reasons: a paraphrase reads very smoothly; most people can read much faster silently than out loud; and everything is so new at first that an attention span of over an hour is common. In a few weeks anyone can have a good foundation for Bible study!

The reading methods need to be suited to their particular purposes. But in general, they are designed to get us reading, and to keep us reading, the whole Bible. I give them one star.

---

*Value rating for each method from 1 to 5 stars.

Study Guides**

The use of study guides for personal Bible study is popular, and I give that system two stars because it brings us into the realm of actual study. Study guides are most beneficial when they are designed to promote and supplement our independent study, and they often do that by modeling the important methods discussed below. If they are used to entirely replace independent study, however, a stifling dependence upon them can result. But many devout men have shared their biblical insights with others through Bible study guides, and as long as we are careful to *prove* their conclusions by independent study, the system will continue to be an important source of help to many believers.

Element Tracing***

Very often we want to know everything that the Bible has to say about *one specific thing*, and so we attempt to trace that one thing through the whole Bible. I give this method three stars because it is the first actual study *method* that we have discussed, and it is based upon the principle of harmony that we discussed in chapter five. I often use it to help resolve questions in my mind, and there is a great variety of elements which can be traced. I have found it beneficial to trace such things as a particular sin (e.g., covetousness), a city (e.g., Bethel), a symbol, a word (word study), a doctrine, a prophecy, a virtue, and the list goes on.

This method presumes a question, and therefore serves the goals of another study. For example, if someone was interested in understanding the Bible's teachings on divorce, he would certainly want to know *everything* it says about such things as adultery and covenant.

The process of tracing an element can be as easy as looking up a word in an exhaustive concordance and examining every reference in its context. But sometimes an element is not directly tied to a single word, and depending upon what it is, more work and other tools will be necessary. But it is often an indispensable step in answering our questions.

Single-Event Projection***

This method, which I also give three stars, is designed to help us grasp the significance of one-time events in scripture. It helps us understand both the harmony and the flow of scripture. For example, at Meribah-Kadesh, Moses sinned. But that one event prevented him from entering the Promised Land and profoundly affects our understanding of such things as holiness, covenant, law and grace. In chapter eight we considered how the single event of creation pervades all of scripture by revealing principles of judgment, authority, God's character, and eternity. The greatest example of all must be the event of Christ's crucifixion and resurrection, and how it projects back deeply into Genesis and all the way through Revelation. Studying single events in this way can uncover some profound truths.

Theme and Principle****

As we see consistency in the teachings and events of scripture, we can begin to recognize themes and principles. For example, in chapter two we mentioned several of the themes which appear in Matthew 12—the mystery of iniquity, the deadness of the Law without the Spirit, and the lack of fellowship between light and darkness (seen in the lack of fellowship between Jesus and the Pharisees). As we study the themes and principles of scripture (we shall reap what we sow, death must precede resurrection, etc.), we become deeply involved with living truth and the ways of God with men.[1] This is the "solid food" of Bible study,[2] so I must give this method *four* stars.

Character Study****

This method focuses on the arena of the Bible's true activity, the heart of man. I therefore give it four stars. In character study, we see why God established David and rejected Saul, why He honored Jacob but not Esau. And we find men and women who can be examples for us to follow; we follow the example of their hearts, their love for God and for truth.

Often, sad but true, we have no living models to follow—no one with the courage of Paul, the servant's heart of Elisha, the desire for God of David. Such people seem scarce today, yet I have found the mere experience of meeting them to be for me a transforming experience. But we needn't be limited by the examples in our local churches. We have the heroes of faith in scripture![3]

One evening as I was reading in Joshua, I was stunned by the reality of the man—his courage, his strength of faith, and the consuming proportions to which his love for God had grown. I knew no man like that. Yet Joshua was not a fable. *He lived*. And by him God led Israel into The Land. I suddenly had a model to follow; it *is* possible to have a godly heart like Joshua, and God will indeed always honor that. What a challenge! Who was I afraid of that this should not be my aim? Or what did I love more that I should not pursue it? I had met Joshua the hero of faith—no longer a mere history, but footprints to follow!

Book Study*****

I have reserved the five stars for one method alone: the book study. Only this method allows us to take full advantage of the *flow* of scripture within a book, whereby we can ultimately understand the divine burden on the heart of its author. And only this divine burden can unite every aspect of a book and give us heaven's foundation for understanding it. But most sacred of all is the fact that God gave a measure of His own heart's burden to each author of scripture; and so as we discover the joys of the author, we are discovering the joys of God, and as we feel the author's grief, we are feeling the grief of God.

Our greatest challenge in Bible study itself, therefore, is to bring every available resource to bear on a book of scripture until we become intimate with it and discover its heavenly cornerstone, deep in God's heart.

It is my hope and prayer that the principles and methods discussed in this book will enable you to draw near to God through scripture, and will encourage you in the faith and in God's new covenant with man through His Son Jesus Christ.

Supplement B

An Excellent Library

What are the materials we need for rich Bible study? Many Christians who are faced with persecution do well with just one book—a Bible, or even a portion of one. They do well because they use it thoroughly and do not take it for granted. We are privileged to have an abundance of excellent resources for Bible study and should take full advantage of this God-given opportunity to get to know scripture. But we needn't fill a room with books to do it. The three principles of Bible study teach us the four categories of materials (one of these categories is *not* books) which are useful in a study library, and a few well-chosen, well-used books can go a long way toward filling them. Two of the categories are necessities, and two are supports. We will discuss them in the order of their importance.

Necessities

1. *Bibles*. In chapter three we discussed how reading from different translations of the Bible can help us overcome the translational barrier and also facilitate inductive study. The most valuable items in any library, therefore,

are several different good translations of scripture. The following are excellent, but not by any means the only good
ones. (I suggest reading carefully the preface to every version you use to become familiar with its purpose. Remember that paraphrases in general are smoother reading but
more freely interpretive than translations.)

Translations
Authorized Version (King James)
New King James Version
Revised Standard Version
New International Version
New American Standard Bible
The Amplified Bible
Concordant Literal—New Testament only
Today's English Version (Good News Bible)
New English Bible

Paraphrases
The Living Bible
The New Testament in Modern English (Phillips)

The Bible is its own best commentary, and I heartily
recommend concentrating one's Bible study in the Bible itself. It is immeasurably better to find the answers to our
questions right in the Bible than to rely on commentaries—more than worth the extra work! It takes time, however, to become familiar enough with scripture to find our
own answers readily. That is why I recommend starting
with a good modern version of the New Testament (I used
J. B. Phillips) and reading it through several times just to
get acquainted with it. (It takes less than twelve hours to
read through it once.) Don't worry about answering every
question that comes up; it's amazing how many questions
answer themselves the second time through! I also consider
it *absolutely essential* that these first readings of the New
Testament be done *before* doing any critical or investigative

study of doctrines, such as evaluating the doctrinal position of a particular church.

2. *A good pair of "walking shoes."* This is the other necessity. Nothing brings more understanding of the scriptures than *obedience* to them—inward obedience as well as outward. Understanding the Bible is taught by the Holy Spirit as a laboratory course, not a lecture course; the *life* of faith and faithfulness is at its very soul.

Supports

3. *Critical aids.* These include primarily concordances, Bible atlases, and Bible dictionaries; and they are designed to help us answer specific questions relating to the first principle of study as discussed in chapters three and four. (The study of biblical languages, archaeology and history further enhances our understanding of those answers, but such are not possible for most of us. Fortunately, Bible atlases and Bible dictionaries provide much of the supportive information gained from those disciplines.) The brief aids appended directly to a Bible may prove inadequate for study purposes, so I recommend single-volume works like *Baker's Bible Atlas* (Baker Book House), the *New American Standard Exhaustive Concordance* (Holman), and *Zondervan Pictorial Bible Dictionary* or *Today's Dictionary of the Bible* (Bethany House). There are many excellent ones to choose from, and hardly a year goes by without a worthy addition to the market. So before buying a new one, I suggest visiting a good Christian bookstore and asking the staff to recommend some.

Commentaries also provide useful background information for the particular passages of scripture they discuss. And they are useful reference works for learning traditional interpretations of difficult passages.

Bible studies are not *critical aids* per se, and like commentaries, they aim primarily at the questions involving the second principle rather than the first. But they serve a very important function in helping new believers discover the basic truths of scripture. Although they can be very beneficial, they must never be allowed to replace personal Bible reading and study.

4. *Devotional aids.* These are designed to help us in the third principle of Bible study. It is in the realm of the third principle that the Bible comes alive. Here its power is released to transform lives; here, the kingdom of God is built. Classics by great men of God such as Andrew Murray and Oswald Chambers have stood the test of time. Devotional aids are intended to support item two above, and never to replace it. As with Bible studies, if they are allowed to diminish our use of either of the two "necessities" above, they no longer support but undermine. How we use our library, therefore, is a primary factor in its effectiveness.

Supplement C

Questions for Group Discussion

These questions are intended to stimulate discussion of the vital concepts in each chapter and to apply those concepts to passages of scripture immediately. Our understanding can be greatly enhanced by sharing our different insights and perspectives in a group. And the immediate application of those concepts further clarifies and solidifies our understanding.

This guide is designed for a series of eight small group meetings (five to thirteen people) of approximately one hour in length. It assumes that the participants have previously read the chapter(s) to be discussed and have given some consideration to the discussion questions. If the number of meetings, meeting length or group size is different, the group leader should adapt the material ahead of time.

Chapter three has a "homework" section on inductive study which is best worked through individually prior to the group meeting. Also notice that the last two meetings cover two chapters each (7-8 and 9-10).

Chapter 1

1. What passages of scripture have deep personal mean-

ing to you, and why have those particular passages become so meaningful to you?

2. Under what circumstances has a passage of scripture effected a permanent change in your life? How did the circumstances contribute to your understanding or application of that passage?

3. Under what circumstances does Bible reading bear little fruit? (Consider Matthew 13:3-23.)

4. What obstacles to their study of the Bible did the young woman and the pastor discussed in this chapter have in common?

5. How do the student and master-level violinists illustrate the essential nature of Bible study?

6. If we want to learn the scriptures intimately and permanently, what should be our specific goal for Bible study? Why?

7. In the light of this chapter, consider Jesus' teaching in Matthew 21:33-41. What was Jesus primarily trying to communicate to the Pharisees? How did He go about doing this? Why?

8. Can you suggest other portions of scripture where the writer or speaker had the same purpose?

Chapter 2

1. What methods of Bible study have you used? Which have been the most beneficial and which have been disappointing? Can you explain the success or failure of any method on the basis of how carefully it incorporated the three principles?

2. Based upon these principles, and the study of chapter one, does any particular method appear to be the most natural or the most important?

3. Which principles would correlate most directly with each of the following words: fact, interpretation, understanding, application, fruit (as in John 15:16)?

4. Can you think of any particular doctrinal question which might be answered by applying these principles? (Be as specific as possible in explaining.)

5. Which principle do you think is most often neglected? Which have you neglected?

6. How could you beneficially change your approach to Bible study based on these three principles?

7. Consider Matthew 22:23-33. Which principle did the Sadducees neglect that led to their error? What principle did the Pharisees neglect in Matthew 23:1-3? In Matthew 12:7?

Chapter 3

1. Can you think of a Bible verse or passage that you had to read many times before you began to understand the author's intended meaning? Why do you think you didn't understand immediately? (Compare experiences in the group.)

2. What is the specific goal of inductive study?

3. What natural barrier does inductive study endeavor to overcome?

4. By comparison, how does that barrier compare with the translational barrier? (How much of our lack of understanding of scripture can be directly attributed to not knowing Greek or Hebrew?)

5. Discuss your results to the inductive study exercise below, or break up into groups of two or three and do the exercise together. Then compare results.

Several years ago, I prepared a study of the second and third chapters of Revelation for a Sunday school class. In my preliminary study, I found that the more observations I made, the more questions I had! As an illustration of inductive study, I invite you to follow me through this exercise.

126

1. *Get some paper and pencil and make as many obser-vations about Revelation 2-3 as you can.*

2. *Let's compare answers.*

I had remembered that there were seven churches and some of the details about them. But it was a new observation for me to notice that there were seven distinct and different promises to those who overcome, one promise to the overcomers in each of the seven churches. The question I then asked was, "How many different things are found seven times, once for each church?" If you have not asked that question and made such a list, take time to do so now.

3. *Let's compare answers again.*

I was surprised to notice seven times the phrase, "He who has an ear, let him hear. . . " and that seven times Christ introduced himself before He spoke, each time differently, based upon His revelation to John in the first chapter (Rev. 1:12-30). I then decided that a chart would be the simplest way to record further observations. The chart grew with my observations, and you will find on the next page a pattern of that chart for you to copy to record yours. If you have not already done so, please do it now.

4. *Study your completed chart and make as many more observations as seem significant.*

5. *Let's compare answers again.*

I noticed a precise correlation between the revelation of Christ given to each church and His admonition to it. I began to meditate also on the rewards to the overcomers and started discovering a correlation there also. Line six was still mostly blank, but as I started recognizing the harmony of the lines within each column, I also started filling in those blanks.

6. *Study your chart to see the harmony within each column and, based upon that harmony, fill in line six as well as you can.* (Line two is largely symbolic. You may find the latter part of chapter four of this book to be helpful.)

7. *Discuss your results on line six with the discussion group.*

1. Church's name	Ephesus	Smyrna	Pergamum	Thyatira	Sardis	Philadelphia	Laodicea
2. The revelation of Christ to the church				1. Son of God 2. Eyes like a flame of fire 3. Feet like burnished bronze.			
3. The condition of the church		In tribulation					
4. The admonition to the church							1. Be zealous 2. Repent
5. The rewards to those who conquer	To eat of the tree of life which is in the midst of the paradise of God.						
6. "He who has an ear, let him hear what the Spirit is saying to the churches." What is the Spirit saying to the churches (us)?			Stop compromising. Then you will discover your true identity in the Kingdom of God and receive its provision.				

8. *Revelation 4:5 and 5:6 might suggest a seventh line for the chart. How would you fill in that line?* (This does not provide a dogmatic answer to the questions raised in those two verses!)

Chapter 4

1. Why did Nicodemus have difficulty accepting the words of Jesus in John 3:3-9? In what ways do we face similar difficulties?

2. What is the difference between spiritual reality and physical reality? How can we retrain our minds to be more receptive to God's truth?

3. What went on in the hearts of the three Hebrews in Daniel 3:14-18? How similar might the circumstances of their dilemma be to circumstances that we face? How similar might their crisis of heart be to crises of heart that we face? To apply this scripture to our own lives then, which is more important, the crisis of heart, or the circumstances which caused the crisis?

4. Consider Exodus 21:18-19 (NASB: ". . . and shall take care of him until he is completely healed"). How would this law, if practiced, affect the hearts of the people involved?

5. Why did Jesus teach in parables? What difficulties did John face in describing his vision in Revelation 1:10-18?

6. Why is symbolic language used in scripture? What are the three basic types of symbolic language used in scripture? Which type of symbolic language has the most consistent interpretation of its symbols? Can you think of any other ways that the Bible expresses spiritual reality in natural terms?

7. How would you classify the symbolism of John 6:48-58? What type of symbolism is used in Exodus 25-27? (For a clue, see Hebrews 9, especially verses 23-24.) Were Jesus and Moses therefore prophets? (Acts 3:20-23; 7:37; Deut. 18:15).

Chapter 5

1. What accounts for the harmony within scripture? What accounts for the harmony of scripture with physical and spiritual reality? (Consider 2 Timothy 3:16.)

2. Discuss Matthew 22:41-46. What caused the apparent contradiction that Jesus pinpointed? Why were the Pharisees unable to answer Christ's question? (Note the irony of Christ himself asking the question!) How should we respond to apparent contradictions in scripture?

3. Discuss the ways that Matthew 22:36-40 can bring harmony to difficult passages of scripture. (Matthew 12:1-8 would be a good test case for this.) In what ways should it bring balance into our practice of the Christian faith?

4. How can we use our understanding of the harmony of scripture as an effective tool for Bible study? List as many ways as you can.

5. Tell of an instance from your personal experience where the harmony of scripture helped you to understand a Bible passage.

Chapter 6

1. Give from your own experience a specific Bible verse whose meaning was clarified for you by comparison with its context, and explain how the context helped.

2. What accounts for the "flow" in any piece of good literature?

3. What accounts for the flow within a single book of scripture such as a New Testament epistle? A gospel? (Answer those questions separately, please.) What does this indicate about *the potential benefit* to us of identifying and understanding the flow of a single book of scripture? Be specific.

4. What accounts for the flow of the Bible as a whole book?

5. Why is it important to understand the author's purpose in his writing? Why is this especially important for us with the writers of scripture? Be *specific*.

6. What are the best indicators of an author's purpose in his writing? What might be indicated when a particular verse or passage doesn't seem to us to fit in with the entire book?

7. List the ways we can use our understanding of the flow of scripture as an effective tool for Bible study. (Keep in mind the main goal of Bible study as discussed in chapter one, specifically questions five and six.)

8. Discuss John 3:20. Briefly explain its apparent meaning taken alone. Find as many additional insights as you can by considering its meaning in the context of the paragraph in which it occurs, verses 16-21.

Chapters 7 and 8

Chapter 7

1. The third principle might be called the principle of personal involvement. Why is personal involvement important in the performance of music? Why does mechanical or intellectual interpretation of music fail to carry the composer's feelings to the heart of the listeners?

2. Discuss 1 Corinthians 3:1. Why were the Christians to whom Paul was writing unable to understand spiritual matters? Was it simply lack of interest, or was it actual inability to comprehend? (Consider also 1 Corinthians 2:14 and 3:2-3.) What can such Christians do to become receptive to deeper spiritual truth, to "solid food" instead of just "milk"?

3. What was God's first relationship with man? What is the first way that God is revealed in the Bible. How important is this to our relationship with Him today?

Chapter 8

4. What was God's purpose in creating man? What was

His purpose in making us in His own image? (Does Genesis 2:18 give us a clue? See also Revelation 22:17—"Bride.")

5. "Then the Lord God called to the man . . . , 'Where are you?' " (Gen. 3:9). From there to the end of the Bible, God is reaching down to man. What aspect of God's nature does this reveal?

6. How do these two aspects of God (creative and redemptive) combine to show us how we must relate to Him?

7. What has God done that we might have a proper relationship to Him? (1 Pet. 1:18-19).

8. What must we do to place ourselves in this relationship? (Rom. 10:9-10). What new beginning do we experience then? (1 Pet. 1:23; John 3:3-8).

9. In what three ways can we know Him personally?

10. Are you experiencing all three aspects of this relationship? If not, what can you do to change that?

Chapters 9 and 10

Chapter 9

1. Which Bible teachers do you enjoy listening to? Why do you think you especially enjoy them? Scholarship? Style of teaching? Personal dedication to Christ and His work?

2. Why is hermeneutics alone unable to keep teachings pure?

3. How does the third principle help us to evaluate teachings that we hear?

4. Is any person able to declare confidently that his heart is incapable of sinning? What does this teach about humility in Bible teaching?

5. In light of all human fallibility, does God still anoint people to be teachers? (1 Cor. 12:28-29). Does a teacher become infallible when he receives an anointing to teach? How, then, are we to respond both to teachers who are called of God and to the teachings they give?

Chapter 10

6. Are there any shortcuts to becoming a master violinist? (If you know of any, do not hesitate. Send them immediately to this author, c/o Bethany House Publishers!)

7. Are there any shortcuts to becoming intimate with God through scripture?

8. Rewrite the first three paragraphs of chapter ten describing Bible study instead of music and using a teacher or preacher in place of Issac Stern. This could be done together as a group, or individually to compare answers afterward. Try to maintain the original wording, making only the necessary changes. Start it something like this: "When you listen to *an anointed man* like *Billy Graham preach from the Bible*, what are you hearing? Is it the. . ." (I don't want to spoil the fun by going too far!)

9. Consider 2 Timothy 2:15, and do the following inductive study exercise. Break up into groups of two or three and list as many one-sentence observations as you can find from that one verse. Be sure that every observation can be substantiated by that verse, and see if you can make valid observations which the other groups will overlook. Take five minutes for this exercise, and then compare results.

10. Which *one thing* that you have learned through these studies (directly or indirectly) do you feel will help you the *most* in your Bible study and your spiritual life overall? (Revealing your answers to this question should be an encouragement to the others in the group.)

Notes

All scripture references, unless otherwise noted, are taken from the *New American Standard Bible* (NASB), published by Creation House, Carol Stream, Illinois. 1960.

Chapter 1
1. Matthew 28:20.
2. 2 Corinthians 10:4; Ephesians 6:17.
3. 2 Timothy 2:15; 3:16-17.

Chapter 2
1. For an excellent analysis of inductive study, I suggest reading William C. Lincoln, *Personal Bible Study* (Minneapolis: Bethany House Publishers, 1975).
2. Psalm 19:7 (KJV).
3. Jude 4; 1 Timothy 6:3-5; Colossians 2:18; Philippians 3:17-19.
4. Matthew 13:11-16.
5. 2 Thessalonians 2:11-12.
6. Luke 24:13-32; John 16:13.

Chapter 3
1. Published by Bethany House Publishers, 1975.

Chapter 4

1. Luke 10:8-11.
2. John 1:51.
3. Psalm 89:14; 97:2.
4. For example, Daniel 12:4, 9.
5. Psalm 12:6; 66:10; Isaiah 4:4; 6:5-7; Malachi 3:2-3; Luke 3:16-17.

Chapter 5

1. Matthew 23:23.
2. Deuteronomy 29:29; Psalm 119:105, etc.
3. Romans 2:15.
4. Matthew 24:22.
5. Titus 3:9.
6. Matthew 7:1-2.

Chapter 6

1. Proverbs 2-3 (especially 3:13-26); Ephesians 2:8; Psalm 25:14.

Chapter 7

1. For example, Hebrews 11:3.
2. 2 Timothy 3:16.
3. Luke 8:15.
4. Deuteronomy 28:8-10.
5. Luke 8:15.
6. Psalm 103:14.
7. Isaiah 6:5-7; 55:2; Micah 6:8; Jeremiah 7:23.
8. Jeremiah 31:31-34.
9. Deuteronomy 6:4-5 and Matthew 22:36-37. Matthew 6:25-34 and Deuteronomy 1:31; 8:5. Exodus 14:31 and John 5:46. Jeremiah 7:23 and Luke 6:46.
10. 2 Samuel 12:13; Isaiah 6:7.
11. Matthew 11:30.
12. See Revelation 4:1-8 and Psalm 96:7-9 (KJV). Personal encounter and experience is the only way to acquire this understanding, and Isaiah the prophet is a case in point

as recorded in Isaiah 6:1-7.

13. Luke 1:72-75.

14. Deuteronomy 5:15. This verse is the clearest statement of God's *intent* with regard to the Sabbath law. It was to remind the Jews that they were *slaves* in bondage, and completely unable to deliver themselves; and that God by His own strength and His own initiative delivered them from that bondage. God wanted them to remember this constantly.

15. Hebrews 4:9-10.

16. Matthew 26:28; John 6:51.

17. Hebrews 7-10.

18. Romans 6:23.

Chapter 8

1. Genesis 3:9.

2. Genesis 3:22-24.

3. Revelation 22:14.

4. 1 Corinthians 15:45-50.

5. 2 Corinthians 12:2-4; Revelation 4:2-6; 10:1-4.

6. Revelation 21:9-27.

7. Psalm 24:1-2.

8. Psalm 81:16.

9. Proverbs 16:25.

10. 1 Corinthians 6:19-20.

11. 1 Peter 1:18-19.

12. Proverbs 1:29-31; Revelation 20:11-15; Isaiah 64:7.

13. Psalm 73:25; Matthew 22:36-38.

14. Jude 21; 1 Thessalonians 2:12; 4:1-12; 2 Thessalonians 1:11-12; Philippians 1:27; Ephesians 4:1. As you consider each of these references in their respective contexts, you may discover that most New Testament teaching is for this purpose: to help us walk in such a way that God's love in its fullest measure can reach us and fill us.

15. Psalm 73:26 (KJV).

16. John 3:1-8; 2 Corinthians 5:17.

17. 1 John 2:1.
18. Deuteronomy 8:16; 30:9.
19. Psalm 139:7-12.
20. Matthew 18:1-6, 10; Luke 10:20.
21. John 17:20-23.
22. Hebrews 11:8-10, 13-16.
23. Mark 4:19.
24. 2 Corinthians 5:7.

Chapter 9

1. Walter Martin has done an admirable job in *The Kingdom of the Cults* (Minneapolis: Bethany House Publishers, 1977).

2. Braden, Charles Samuel, Ph.D., *The Scriptures of Mankind,* The Macmillan Co., 1952, pp. 474-476.

3. Braden, p. 480.

4. Martin, pp. 63-100.

5. From the preface to the 1944 edition. See also Braden, pp. 477-479.

6. Braden, pp. 474-476.

7. Titus 1:9-11. Notice that the overseer (v. 7) must deal with *both* the doctrine and with the persons who are responsible for contradicting. Verse 11 identifies a common root sin.

8. 2 Corinthians 11:3.

9. Titus 1:7-11.

10. Colossians 3:14.

11. 1 John 5:21.

12. 1 Corinthians 4:4-5.

13. Matthew 22:37.

14. Romans 10:10.

Chapter 10

1. Hebrews 4:2 (note context).
2. Luke 10:38-42 (cf. John 11:1).
3. Romans 12:1 (KJV).

Supplements

1. Psalm 103:7.
2. 1 Corinthians 3:2; Hebrews 5:12-14.
3. Hebrews 11.